W9-BSP-521

Managing Your Depression

A JOHNS HOPKINS PRESS HEALTH BOOK

SASKATOON PUBLIC LIBRARY
36001401116867 RM
Managing your depression : what

Managing *Your* DEPRESSION

What You Can Do to Feel Better

Susan J. Noonan, M.D., M.P.H.

Foreword by Timothy J. Petersen, Ph.D.,
Jonathan E. Alpert, M.D., Ph.D.,
and Andrew A. Nierenberg, M.D.

THE JOHNS HOPKINS UNIVERSITY PRESS *Baltimore*

Note to the reader: The information in this book should by no means be considered a substitute for the advice of qualified medical professionals. Mental diseases and disorders have a wide range of symptoms and clinical presentations. You should always consult qualified medical professionals for the diagnosis and treatment of mental diseases and disorders. All efforts have been made to ensure the accuracy of the information contained in this book as of the date of publication. The author and the publisher expressly disclaim responsibility for any adverse outcomes arising from the use or application of the information contained herein.

If you are thinking about suicide, you should immediately contact your health care provider, go to the nearest Emergency Department, or call 9-1-1.

© 2013 The Johns Hopkins University Press
All rights reserved. Published 2013
Printed in the United States of America on acid-free paper
9 8 7 6 5 4 3 2 1

The Johns Hopkins University Press
2715 North Charles Street
Baltimore, Maryland 21218-4363
www.press.jhu.edu

Library of Congress Cataloging-in-Publication Data
Noonan, Susan J., 1953–
Managing your depression : what you can do to feel better / Susan J. Noonan, M.D., M.P.H. ; foreword by Timothy J. Petersen, Ph.D., Jonathan E. Alpert, M.D., Ph.D., and Andrew A. Nierenberg, M.D.
pages cm
Includes bibliographical references and index.
ISBN 978-1-4214-0946-7 (hardcover : alk. paper)
ISBN 978-1-4214-0947-4 (pbk. : alk. paper)
ISBN 978-1-4214-0948-1 (electronic)
ISBN 1-4214-0946-1 (hardcover : alk. paper)
ISBN 1-4214-0947-X (pbk. : alk. paper)
ISBN 1-4214-0948-8 (electronic)
1. Depression, Mental. 2. Self-care, Health. I. Title.
RC537.N66 2013
616.85'27—dc23 2012036701

A catalog record for this book is available from the British Library.

Special discounts are available for bulk purchases of this book. For more information, please contact Special Sales at 410-516-6936 or specialsales@press.jhu.edu.

The Johns Hopkins University Press uses environmentally friendly book materials, including recycled text paper that is composed of at least 30 percent post-consumer waste, whenever possible.

Contents

Tables and Forms

Tables

Forms

Foreword

About as many millions of individuals suffer from mood disorders in any given year as from cancer or diabetes. Among all medical conditions worldwide, mood disorders are recognized by the World Health Organization as among the most disabling. By affecting all domains of functioning, including sleep, appetite, energy, mood, motivation, self-esteem, judgment, and hopefulness, major depressive disorder and bipolar disorder interfere with the ability to work, study, maintain relationships, and carry on the very activities of daily living. Social isolation, poor self-care, and pessimism, core symptoms of depression, often become part of a pernicious cycle further reinforcing the impact of a mood disorder on an individual and on families and communities. The most devastating outcome of mood disorders is suicide, which occurs at a tragic rate of about one every 15 minutes in the United States. Although mood disorders, particularly depression, have been thought of in terms of individual episodes of illness, they have increasingly been recognized as often relapsing/remitting conditions that may extend over many years and benefit greatly from astute management through a collaboration between clinician and patient.

Fortunately, over the last three decades, a great deal has been learned about the effective treatment of mood disorders. Evidence-based medication and psychotherapeutic approaches along with novel pharmacological and nonpharmacological treatment strategies have improved our ability to manage illness acutely and prevent recurrence. We continue to learn more about the neurobiological and environmental contributions to mood disorders and how individualized factors may inform treatment choice. Compelling research efforts are underway to investigate the best ways to combine treatment approaches as well as how to prevent the onset of illness in those at risk but not yet affected. Given the prevalence, impact, and often long-term course of major depressive disorder and bipolar disorder, the value of effective treatment, persistence, and well-informed, engaged patients and families in the optimal management of mood disorders is all the more apparent.

In this book, Dr. Noonan courageously presents "lessons learned" during her years of combating a mood disorder. In stark contrast to a model in which patients are passive recipients of diagnosis and treatment, we hope readers will appreciate the overarching theme presented: the critical importance of *proactively managing mental health*. Dr. Noonan offers the reader comprehensive and accessible coverage of key concepts and principles that are translated into practical "ready to use" self-management skills. Among the book's outstanding accomplishments are:

- Inclusion of easy-to-read, accurate descriptions of signs and symptoms of mood disorder diagnoses
- Review of medication treatment strategies with an emphasis on how to promote open dialogue between providers and patients
- Presentation of graphic tools for use in tracking symptoms and challenging maladaptive thoughts and behaviors

Perhaps most impressive is the thorough coverage given to skills steeped in the tradition of cognitive and behaviorally based psychotherapies. These skills are predicated on the well-known fact that the way in which an individual *thinks* and *behaves* predictably changes during the course of a mood disorder. When depressed, an individual sees the world as half empty and selects for elements of the environment that support this negative view. Alternatively, while hypomanic or manic, an individual can view the world and himself or herself in an overly optimistic or even grandiose manner. Behaviors corresponding to these mood states include isolation/withdrawal and impulsivity/risk taking, respectively. Dr.

Noonan's book offers pragmatic and insightful methods to address *both* thoughts and behaviors altered during one's struggle with a mood disorder.

It is an honor to have worked with Dr. Noonan during her long battle with depression. As we hope Dr. Noonan has learned from us, we have learned much from her and incorporate these insights into our work with others. This book is emblematic of Dr. Noonan's persistence, courage, expertise, willingness to disclose, and desire to share with others practical ways to successfully cope with and manage a mood disorder. We thank her for a contribution that will undoubtedly enhance the health and quality of life of many readers.

Timothy J. Petersen, Ph.D.
Jonathan E. Alpert, M.D., Ph.D.
Andrew A. Nierenberg, M.D.
The Massachusetts General Hospital
Department of Psychiatry
Boston, Massachusetts

Acknowledgments

This book is dedicated to a team of exceptional people who have made my life and this book possible. The superior clinical skills, extraordinary kindness, understanding, and perseverance of these professionals have been invaluable and have kept hope alive for me when I believed there was none. I owe my deepest thanks and gratitude to Drs. Andrew Nierenberg, Jonathan Alpert, Timothy Petersen, John Winkelman, Karen Carlson, and David Mischoulon. Additional thanks and appreciation go to Drs. Jeffery Huffman, Michelle Jacobo, and Marc Zuckerman for knowing just what to say and do during the darkest moments and for keeping me safe during those times. Last, I would like to recognize the remarkably skilled and caring nursing staff of Blake 11 for exceeding all expectations.

My family, father and brother, have been particularly generous and supportive in their own way, and for that I am most grateful. And my friends are the ones who have sustained me throughout. They deserve the highest praise for strength in friendship over a lifetime marked with a fluctuating illness. Special thanks and appreciation go to Sandi, Bernice, Eileen, Ginger, JoAnn, Cindy, Joe, Dave, David, and Carlo for their dear friendship and support.

No book is published alone, and the amazing, insightful team of Jacqueline Wehmueller and staff of the Johns Hopkins University Press deserve special recognition, including Juliana McCarthy, Kathy Alexander, Claire McCabe Tamberino, and Sara Cleary. I would also like to extend my thanks and appreciation to copyeditor Melanie Mallon for her perceptive and thoughtful care of the manuscript.

Managing Your Depression

Introduction

Some call it the blues or a storm in their head. William Styron called it darkness visible. Whatever the description, depression is a disorder of the mind and body that affects approximately 15 percent of the population at some point in their lives. Mood disorders such as major depression and bipolar disorder are conditions of the brain that involve a disturbance in one's mood or frame of mind. These conditions affect a person's thoughts, feelings, behaviors, relationships, activities, interests, and other aspects of life. It can be quite overwhelming. The symptoms of major depression and bipolar disorder are often remitting and relapsing. This means that the symptoms come and go; they may improve or go away and then return at some later time. The pattern is unique for each person and difficult to predict. You may experience symptoms for a long time, just as people who have diabetes or high blood pressure often do. The important thing to remember is that mood disorders are treatable and that you can learn to manage yours.

One of the most common symptoms of major depression and bipolar disorder is difficulty with concentration and focus. In his book, Styron eloquently described a state of confusion, failure of mental focus, lapse of memory, and muddied thought processes, familiar to many with depression. This may make it challenging for you to read, pay attention to a conversation or TV show, or remember simple things. Although advice on how to manage a mood disorder can be found in many textbooks, self-help books, and Web sites, a person with depression may find some of these resources difficult to follow and absorb. Books and articles with long, involved text can be overwhelming to a person in the midst of depression. These are symptoms of the disease, not indications of your intelligence. Because of these symptoms, learning to manage depression requires a different approach.

Managing Your Depression was designed with this idea in mind. Its main focus is on practical, day-to-day ways to manage your illness. The book provides you with core information in a concise form. It is brief and to the point. The basics of managing your depression or bipolar disorder are broken down into several sections, with skill sets and exercises that can be done one at a time. My perspective in writing is that of a physician who has treated many patients and who also has personal experience living with the illness. Having been in the depths of a mood disorder, I have an understanding of what information is most helpful to manage the illness and how it is best received.

The information presented here was gathered over time from various educational resources, psychoeducational programs, seminars, expert health care providers, and personal patient experience. If you suffer from mood disorders, you can use this book as:

- an educational source to better understand and manage your illness. You need to have specific knowledge and skills to respond to an illness like depression so that you can avoid its worsening, recover, and prevent recurrences. Managing your mood disorder in an informed way can help you function better and stay well. People who participate actively in their own care and who work to manage their mood disorder have a better chance of recovery and of staying well.
- a workbook, a set of skills and exercises to use along with input, advice, and treatment from your therapist and treatment team. This book is not intended to replace your treatment professional(s).

The reader is advised to go slowly. Review one section at a time and keep in mind that you may need to review it more than once. People with depression have various clinical signs and symptoms in a pattern that is unique to each of them. Look for the material that applies to your own experiences over time. You may find some of the exercises to be starting points for discussions in your therapy sessions. Work with your therapist to determine the most helpful educational and exercise tools for you. It's worth repeating—people who participate actively in their care have a better chance of recovery and staying well.

I begin in chapter 1 with the mental health basics, the essential things we all need to do daily to maintain emotional health and stability. The basic steps include maintaining a regular pattern of sleep, diet, exercise, medications, and social contacts; keeping a routine and structure to your day; and avoiding isolation. These fundamentals can be especially challenging when you are managing a mood disorder because the symptoms of depression often interfere with your ability to do them.

In the second chapter, I give an overview of the mood disorders called major depression and bipolar disorder. This chapter also includes a brief discussion of depression in women, depression and anxiety, the stigma of mood disorders, and fatigue and depression. There is a comprehensive table of the real-life symptoms of major depression and bipolar disorder and a daily Mood Chart to track your symptoms.

Chapter 3 presents the concept of *defining your baseline*. Your baseline is your healthy inner self, something that appears to be lost during severe depression, even if only temporarily. In managing depression, you have to find a way to stay connected to your baseline healthy person, your inner sense of yourself. This baseline can be extraordinarily helpful to draw on during your recovery. This chapter also includes exercises to help you identify and define your baseline self.

Chapter 4 begins with an overview of treatment for mood disorders and your relationship with your therapist, followed by what you need to know to manage your depression and bipolar disorder. It is important to use both professional treatment and self-management techniques to achieve the best recovery from your illness. Managing depression means that you learn about the illness and its symptoms and develop effective strategies to respond to your symptoms. It requires that you monitor your symptoms, challenge negative thoughts, use problem-solving techniques, make adjustments, and avoid negative behaviors.

In chapter 5, you will find an overview of Relapse Prevention. Relapse Prevention is an effective daily approach to help you minimize the chance of a relapse (return of symptoms) and help you stay well. This chapter also provides ways to help you identify your depression Warning Signs and Triggers and an intervention Action Plan for Relapse Prevention to use when an important change in your emotional health happens.

Chapter 6 is a presentation of cognitive behavioral therapy (CBT), a specific type of talk therapy that addresses the connection between your thoughts, feelings, and behaviors. CBT is particularly useful in depression when your thoughts are distorted, negative, and causing you distress. This form of therapy helps to identify and change distorted thinking patterns, inaccurate beliefs, and unhelpful behaviors that are common in depression. Included here are sample CBT exercises for you to use to challenge and change dysfunctional thinking patterns.

I explore in chapter 7 some life strategies to get you through the tough times. These skills often fade during depression, so you may need to review and polish up on them. This chapter covers Coping and Stress, Mindfulness, Distress Tolerance, Communication Skills, Dealing with Family and Friends, Talking with Your Doctor, and Tips for Families and Friends.

Chapter 8 describes how it looks and feels to manage your depression by incorporating the recommendations throughout this book into your daily life. Chapter 9 is a collection of thoughtful advice and resources for your review, including reliable and recommended Internet sites and books of interest. Next is a concluding chapter, which is rounded out by references, a glossary of important terms used in the book, and an index.

CHAPTER 1

Mental Health Basics

The Basic Steps

The Basics of Mental Health are the essential actions we all need to engage in every day to maintain emotional health and stability. They are especially important when you are trying to manage a mood disorder. The basic steps include maintaining a regular pattern of sleep, a healthy diet, and regular physical exercise; taking prescribed medications; keeping up social contacts; and having a routine and structure to your day. The steps are your foundation for a healthy emotional life, and on them you will build the components of your treatment plan. These may feel like common sense recommendations, but they are essential to controlling your symptoms. Controlling your symptoms in this way improves the quality of your life. When you follow these steps regularly, you will decrease your vulnerability to fluctuations, or changes, in your mood disorder symptoms. Taking care of your overall self is important to your general health and to preserving your emotional balance and strength. It also boosts your resilience. This helps you to recover more quickly from setbacks or episodes of depression if they do occur.

Following these fundamental steps can be especially challenging when you are struggling to manage a mood disorder because the symptoms of depression often interfere with your ability to actually do them. For example, the symptoms of fatigue, poor appetite, and lack of interest can make it difficult to do the grocery shopping and cooking necessary to follow a healthy diet. To meet this challenge, you may find it helpful to break down the tasks of daily life into small steps, to plan for what you have to do, and to

The Basics of Mental Health

- Treat any physical illness.
- Sleep
  - Aim for 7 to 8 hours of sleep each night.
  - Keep a regular sleep routine.
  - Follow Sleep Hygiene principles to promote restorative, restful sleep.
  - Use a Sleep Diary to track sleep patterns.
- Diet and nutrition
  - Eat balanced, healthy meals regularly, 3 times a day.
  - Do not use alcohol, street drugs, or excessive caffeine.
- Medications
  - Take all medications as prescribed, even if you are feeling better.
  - Discuss with your physician all over-the-counter medications, herbs, and other supplements you take.
- Exercise regularly (as able); balance cardiovascular, stretch, and strengthening activities.
- Maintain regular social contacts and connections with others.
- Avoid isolation.
- Have a daily routine and structure your time.

pace yourself. In the current example, you could write down your grocery list, shop at a time of day when you have more energy, and cook healthy foods in large batches so that you can freeze some for later meals when you are too fatigued to cook. You will learn more about these techniques in the following chapters. The key is not to wait until you feel like doing something. Just do it as best as you can now and the motivation for doing it will follow. Many people with depression have found that to be so. It is crucial that you keep trying despite the difficulty and that you give yourself credit for the effort.

The Basics of Mental Health are summarized on page 6. A more detailed discussion of these steps follows below.

Sleep and Depression

Sleep problems often occur during an episode of major depression or bipolar disorder. When depressed, you may sleep a lot but still feel tired. You may sleep too little or have interrupted sleep, with frequent awakenings during the night. Or you may wake up too early. The quality of your sleep may be affected so that you don't feel rested or restored the next day. Without enough sleep you become irritable and have difficulty concentrating and doing small tasks. In contrast, in bipolar disorder with mania or hypomania you may feel that you don't need very much sleep at all, that you are energized and awake during normal sleep times.

Why does sleep matter to your mental health? Sound sleep optimizes brain function and has a positive effect on your mood disorder. A change in the amount or quality of sleep will affect your illness. For example, periods of insufficient or poor-quality sleep can worsen your depression or bring on your bipolar illness. A consistent period of good night's sleep can help improve your mood.

Changes in your sleep may or may not be fully under your control. They may be related to a physical condition or stress. Sleep difficulties may be Warning Signs or Symptoms of your mood disorder, which you and your treatment team can recognize and address. Sleep disruption may also be related to environmental conditions, such as noise level, excess light, or extremes in room temperature. The good news is that you can control some things to help yourself achieve a good night's sleep. This is called Sleep Hygiene.

Sleep Hygiene

Sleep Hygiene refers to the personal habits and environmental (home) conditions that affect your sleep. Good sleep habits can help improve your sleep, which in turn will help improve your mood. So it is important to maintain good sleep habits and a consistent sleeping and waking pattern in a bedroom environment that favors sound sleep. Sleep Hygiene recommendations, adapted from the American Academy of Sleep Medicine, are listed below. One of the essential steps in managing your mood disorder is to follow these recommendations as best as you can. Speak with your doctor if you are still having sleep problems after following these suggestions.

Sleep Hygiene

Recommendations to improve your sleep include:

- Keep the same bedtime and wake-up time every day, including weekends. Set an alarm clock if necessary. Get up and out of bed at the same time even if you've had a bad night's sleep.
- Avoid napping during the day.
- Develop a relaxing sleep ritual before bedtime. Create downtime in the last 2 hours before going to bed, and avoid overstimulation, such as family arguments, excess noise, vigorous activity, or violent TV shows or video games.
- Try going to bed only when you are sleepy.
- Avoid watching the clock. Turn the clock away from you.
- Avoid lying in bed unable to fall asleep and feeling frustrated. If you are not asleep after 20 to 30 minutes, get out of bed. Relax and distract your mind with a quiet activity in another room (music, reading), then return to bed when you are sleepy.
- Relaxation exercises before bedtime may be helpful. Examples include progressive muscle relaxation, deep breathing, guided imagery, yoga, or meditation.

- Designate a specific "worry time" earlier in the day or evening to sort out problems you may have. Writing down reminders for the next day is a good way to clear your mind before bed.
- Use your bed and bedroom only for sleep, sex, or occasional illness. Eliminate nonsleep activities in bed, using another room for reading, watching TV, working, and eating.
- Limit how much caffeine you have during the day, and avoid its use after 12:00 noon. Note that coffee, tea, colas, cocoa, chocolate, and some medications contain caffeine.
- Avoid or limit the use of nicotine (tobacco) and alcohol during the day and avoid their use within 4 to 6 hours of bedtime.
- Avoid large meals before bedtime, but do not go to bed hungry. If needed, have a light snack.
- Exercise regularly. Avoid strenuous exercise within 4 to 6 hours of bedtime.
- Create a bedroom environment that favors sound sleep. A comfortable bed in a dark, quiet room is recommended. Minimize light, noise, and extremes in room temperature (hot or cold) in the bedroom. Room-darkening shades, curtains, earplugs, or a sound machine may be helpful.
- Speak with your physician if you are having continued difficulty with sleep, including falling asleep, staying asleep, and early or frequent awakenings.

Source: Adapted in part from the American Academy of Sleep Medicine, "Sleep Hygiene: The Healthy Habits of Good Sleep" (AASM, 2010), www.yoursleep.aasmnet.org/hygiene.aspx, accessed April 2012.

What is enough sleep? The amount of sleep required by a person depends in part on age. It varies from infancy, through childhood, to older age. The average amount of sleep required by healthy adults is 7 to 8 hours per night. "Enough sleep" is the amount that makes you feel physically and mentally rested, sharp, not irritable, and able to concentrate, focus, and correctly do small motor tasks.

How do you know how much sleep you are really getting, and what your sleep patterns are? Most people tend to underestimate the amount of sleep they had. One way to know is to keep track of your sleep for several weeks with a Sleep Diary (pages 12–13). A Sleep Diary is a chart where you record

- your bedtime
- how long it took to get to sleep
- the number of times you woke up during the night
- how long you stayed awake (duration of awakening)
- the time you are finally awake and out of bed in the morning

Fill it out first thing in the morning for several weeks and then share it with your doctor(s). Keeping a Sleep Diary helps you and your treatment team understand your sleep patterns. It is used to track your progress and response to therapy, and it provides valuable information used in making treatment decisions. It also helps you to stick with good Sleep Hygiene habits.

Diet and Nutrition

You have probably heard that it is important to eat a nutritious and varied diet to keep your body and vital organs working properly. Did you know that this is also true for your brain? Food is the fuel that keeps your body and your brain functioning optimally. Eating well-balanced healthy meals is one way of taking care of yourself that you have control over. It can make a positive difference in your mental health. When you stray from a healthy, regular diet you become vulnerable to mood changes. You may become irritable and fatigued, and your brain may not function very well.

Several research studies have shown an association between particular eating patterns and mental health. For example, a "western diet" high in saturated fats and processed, fried, and sugary foods was found to be associated with a high rate of depression.

In contrast, a diet high in fruits, vegetables, nuts, legumes, fish, whole grains, and olive oil, also known as the Mediterranean diet, was associated with a lower rate of depression. It is not known whether a poor-quality diet is a result of the appetite changes and inertia that accompany depression or whether it causes those symptoms—perhaps both are true. Other studies have shown the significance of the supplements folate, vitamin B12, and omega-3 fatty acids in the diet, but this is a complex discussion that I will not go into here. Talk with your doctor about whether you need to take any of these as dietary supplements for your depression.

A healthy eating pattern is valuable for additional reasons. Improving your brain's nutritional status may increase the effectiveness of antidepressant medications. Depression, lack of activity, sleep problems, and many medications prescribed for mood disorders have the potential to increase body weight. Symptoms of depression include loss of appetite and weight loss in some people, while others may have increased appetite, carbohydrate cravings, and weight gain. Weight gain following antidepressant therapy may be an indication of recovery in those who had weight loss as a symptom, or it may be related to taking the medication. Weight gain is a relatively common problem during acute or long-term treatment with antidepressants and is a significant reason people stop taking their medications. Be mindful of this possibility, particularly if you are on medication for the long term.

Significant weight gain related to taking antidepressant medications can affect your overall health and cause physical and emotional discomfort and distress. Many people feel worse about themselves, having low self-esteem and low confidence, when they gain substantial weight. Healthy eating may prevent or reduce the likelihood of becoming overweight or obese while on these medications. Those already overweight will have to control their total caloric intake to manage their body weight. This is only part of the picture. Controlling your weight also means increasing physical activity (exercise) and decreasing the amount of time spent sitting around. This is not easy to do, but you can take steps to make it

SLEEP DIARY

Date	Bedtime	SOL* (time it takes to fall asleep)	Number of times you woke up during the night	How long, total, were you awake during the night?	Latest time awake	What time did you get out of bed?	Total time asleep
Monday							
Tuesday							
Wednesday							
Thursday							
Friday							
Saturday							
Sunday							

Source: Adapted from National Institutes of Health, National Heart, Lung, and Blood Institute, Your Guide to Healthy Sleep (NHLBI, 2011), www.nhlbi.nih.gov/health/public/sleep, accessed April 2012.
*SOL = sleep onset latency

Did you nap during the day? For how long?	Medications			Exercise	Notes / medication changes

less difficult, as I discuss in the Physical Exercise section of this chapter. Remember that different antidepressant medications all have different effects on your metabolism, so you should remain open to trying more than one drug (if necessary) until you find one that you tolerate well.

Since you have control over what you eat, it is in your best interest to nourish your brain in the most beneficial way. To help you improve your eating habits and reach the goal of a healthy, balanced diet, I have included basic nutritional information in the sections that follow.

What Is a Balanced, Nutritious Diet?

A comprehensive and easy-to-use resource is the USDA *Dietary Guidelines for Americans 2010*. These are evidence-based nutritional guidelines designed to promote health, reduce the risk of chronic diseases, and reduce overweight and obesity through improved nutrition and physical activity. The guidelines are not specific to depression but address general health and well-being. They can be found online at www.health.gov/DietaryGuidelines/ (click on the link to the "policy document").

The *Dietary Guidelines 2010* describe a healthy diet as one that:

- emphasizes fruits, vegetables, whole grains, and fat-free or low-fat milk and milk products;
- includes lean meats, poultry, fish, beans, eggs, and nuts; and
- is low in saturated fats, trans fats, cholesterol, salt (sodium), and added sugars.

You may have seen these recommendations drawn as a food pyramid in the past. The guidelines now display healthy food as portions divided on a dinner plate, with fruits, vegetables, grains, lean protein (such as chicken or fish), and a small amount of dairy. There is an easy-to-use interactive Web site to help you understand the food portions at www.choosemyplate.gov. Visit this Web site for many helpful tips on healthy eating, including menu choices and specific calorie goals for your age and gender. Optimal caloric intake depends on your gender, age, your current weight, and your goals for maintaining, losing or gaining weight. I will not go into that here.

The *Dietary Guidelines 2010* recommend that you make half your plate fruits and vegetables, or that you eat five ½ cup servings of colorful fruits and vegetables per day. The protein portion for adults is 5 to 6 ounces total per day, or approximately one-quarter of your plate at each meal. Grains should be two 3-ounce servings per day for active adults, or approximately one-quarter of your plate. Dairy should be low fat and used in moderation.

Eating for energy and balanced mental health means that you have 3 small to medium meals per day plus two healthy snacks as you choose. Do not skip meals. A snack might be a piece of fruit, or string cheese and a few walnuts or almonds, but no chips, fries, candy, soda, or junk food. You should stay well hydrated by drinking 6 to 8 glasses of water per day. Avoid sugary drinks and diet soda. Avoid alcohol, as it is a depressant and not good for your general physical and mental health. Avoid tobacco and street drugs. If necessary, take one multivitamin supplement per day, but do this with the advice of your doctor. Remember, a balanced, healthy diet leaves you satisfied and not hungry for more.

Pay attention to portion sizes at home and when you eat out, because they have inappropriately increased in size over the years at restaurants and in the home. For example, a healthy serving of protein such as meat or fish is actually 3 ounces, about the size of a deck of cards. A serving (½ cup) of fresh fruit is about the size of half a baseball. One cup of cereal (a serving) is the size of your fist. One serving of rice, pasta, or potato is ½ cup, about the size of half a baseball. (See the NHLBI "Serving Size Card" at http://hp2010.nhlbihin.net/portion/servingcard7.pdf.)

USDA 2010 Dietary Guidelines for Americans

This list summarizes the key points in maintaining a healthy body and weight.

- Increase whole grains, vegetables, and fruits in your diet.
- Eat a variety of vegetables, especially beans, peas, and dark green, red, and orange vegetables.
- Eat at least half of all grains as whole grains. Increase whole-grain intake by replacing refined grains with whole grains.
- Choose a variety of protein foods, which include seafood, lean meat and poultry, eggs, beans and peas, soy products, and unsalted nuts and seeds. Choose a variety of seafood in place of some meat and poultry.
- Use lean, lower-calorie protein foods instead of high-fat protein.
- Reduce the amount of sugar-sweetened beverages you drink.
- Focus on the total number of calories consumed. Monitor your food intake.
- Be aware of portion size: choose smaller portions or lower-calorie options.
- Eat a nutrient-dense breakfast.
- Limit daily sodium (salt) intake to less than 2,300 milligrams (mg) per day.
- Eat less than 10 percent of calories from saturated fatty acids by replacing them with monounsaturated and polyunsaturated fatty acids.
- Eat less than 300 mg per day of dietary cholesterol.
- Increase fat-free or low-fat milk and milk products, such as milk, yogurt, cheese, or fortified soy beverages.
- Use oils to replace solid fats when possible.
- Choose foods that provide more potassium, dietary fiber,

calcium, and vitamin D. These include vegetables, fruits, whole grains, and low-fat milk and milk products.

- Limit foods that contain synthetic sources of trans fats, such as partially hydrogenated oils.

Source: U.S. Department of Agriculture, U.S. Department of Health and Human Services, *Dietary Guidelines for Americans 2010*, 7th edition (Washington, DC, December 2010), www.cnpp.usda.gov/Publications/DietaryGuidelines/2010/PolicyDoc/PolicyDoc.pdf, accessed April 2012.

You have to work hard to build a healthy eating pattern—it does not come naturally to many people. When you are depressed, it is much easier to eat take-out and prepared foods that are higher in fats and salt and not as healthy for you. Grocery shopping and cooking may seem overwhelming, but try to remind yourself how important it is for your mental and physical health. You may find it easier to stick to a healthy diet when you plan ahead. Do this at times of the day when you have the most energy. First, make a shopping list of healthy foods for the grocery store. There are Web sites that can help you with easy menu planning. Try to go shopping at times when it is least crowded and you are not hungry, and if possible, bring a friend along to help you. Many markets have a salad bar with healthy choices to start—just watch the amount of salad dressing you use. Cook soups, stews, or chicken in large batches so that you can freeze portions for later use, on days when fatigue sets in. Buy vegetables and throw them in a crock pot to cook all day—the result is a healthy, nourishing meal with little effort! Cook on days or times of day when you have more energy, or ask a friend to help you do it together. Make your grocery shopping and cooking part of your weekly routine and schedule them in. Some people find that a weekend day is the best time for them to shop and cook for the week. Then just do it even if you do not really feel like it.

Some people experience anxiety along with their depression, and with this they may have unusual food cravings and a tendency to snack on junk food. Try to resist this temptation. Have only healthy foods and snacks at home to reach for when the urge is there. Bring a healthy snack with you to work and have it readily available. A piece of fruit, yogurt, or 12 walnuts or almonds are far better choices than chips or candy. Talk to your doctor if unusual food cravings persist. Keep variety in your diet as a way to ensure your body gets the many nutrients it needs. Variety also helps keep you from getting bored with the same old menus. Try a cooking class. This will also get you out of the house and introduce you to new people and new ideas, which are good for your depression.

Eating out at restaurants can also sabotage the best intentions of maintaining a healthy diet and weight. Try to stick to your plan of portion control, limiting fats and salt. Order an appetizer and salad instead of a main course, request that the salad dressing or sauce be put on the side, share a main course, or ask for a doggy-bag to bring the rest of your entrée home for the next day.

If following a healthy diet and regular exercise program does not solve your weight-gain problem, speak with your physician about alternative medications for depression and sleep. Other options include joining a support group plan such as Weight Watchers, getting a referral to the Weight Center at your local hospital, or speaking with your physician about a medication to help counteract the weight-gaining potential of the antidepressant medications.

Physical Exercise

You have often heard that physical exercise is good for your body and overall health. Did you know that it is also good for your brain, in particular that exercise can alleviate depression?

The benefits of physical exercise as a treatment for depression are that it

- promotes the growth of new brain cells and regulates brain chemicals (neurotransmitters)
- helps to keep the level of stress hormones normal and relieves stress

- increases feelings of confidence, self-esteem, competence, and sense of mastery
- has a positive effect on your mood
- improves your sense of well-being
- releases the "feel good" hormones (endorphins)
- improves the quality of your sleep, which in turn improves your mood disorder
- helps to overcome the inertia and sedentary lifestyle that often comes with depression
- increases your social contacts (in an exercise class or in neighborhood or health club interactions)
- builds endurance and physical strength, which combats fatigue
- helps manage your weight

Regular physical exercise may be helpful alone or when used in addition to standard antidepressant treatment. This is called an *augmentation strategy.* Exercise is also considered part of a Relapse Prevention plan (page 71) and may be associated with lower relapse rates. It is also a way for you to take a more active role in managing your depression. Before beginning an exercise program, discuss your plan with your physician. Mention any physical health concerns, such as heart disease or bone or joint problems.

Depression symptoms may make it more difficult to start and stick with an exercise program. These symptoms include loss of interest in activities, decreased physical and mental energy, decreased motivation, and loss of focus and concentration. However, there are effective steps you can take to deal with these challenges. First, choose an exercise activity that you enjoy, or used to enjoy, and can do regularly. Once you pick your exercise program, sticking with it is the most important part. How do you do that when you are depressed? Make it part of your daily routine and schedule it as a key part of your day. Here is where action precedes motivation. This means that you should start your exercise program now and keep at it, even if you don't really feel like doing it. The motivation for doing it will come later.

If you have not exercised in a while, start slow and gradually build up your time and effort. Commit to walking around the block for 10 minutes each day, and then gradually increase the amount of time you walk each week. Or start by walking 10 minutes away from your house, and then 10 minutes back home, and gradually increase your time. You may want to purchase an inexpensive step counter, a small plastic device you clip to your waist that counts each step as you go about your daily life. The goal is to add 1,000 steps in the course of your day, so that you eventually walk up to 10,000 steps daily. Incorporate small changes into your daily activities, such as walking more places, taking the stairs instead of the elevator, or getting off the subway or bus two stops earlier.

Get Started and Keep It Going

- Do what you enjoy or used to enjoy. Do something that is fun.
- Assess what type of exercise resources are available to you. Look for a safe area to walk in your neighborhood. Find out if there is a community center or health club facility available to you with exercise classes or equipment. Consider whether you have or can invest in home exercise equipment. See what kind of social supports are available to keep you motivated to exercise.
- Plan a specific and realistic activity that you can do. Define the type of activity, how often you will do it, and for how long (frequency and duration).
- Make exercise a priority in your day and a key part of your daily routine.
- Believe that the exercise will have benefit for you—this will make it easier to do.
- List the pros and cons of exercising compared to having a sedentary lifestyle.

- Come up with your own personal reasons for exercising.
- Exercise with a partner (a walking partner or join a class)—you will have to be accountable to him or her to show up and exercise together. This is a good social support.
- Consider having a personal trainer help you set up a program, then monitor and motivate you.
- Identify and address any barriers ahead of time, such as the time of day, your energy level, balancing other obligations, too busy, too tired, too sick, bored, embarrassed, and so forth.
- Work toward a goal that has personal meaning. This could be a walking or running distance or length of time, or a specific exercise accomplishment.
- Train for a charity event (such as a walk, run, bike ride).
- Track your progress in a journal or log and review it periodically.
- Focus on the activity and not on your performance. Try not to make comparisons to your past or to others' performance.
- As you get stronger, vary your activity so that you avoid boredom and repetitive injury.
- Give yourself credit for what you can do now.

Exercise Guidelines

What counts as exercise? Exercise is any physical activity or movement of the body that uses energy. The American College of Sports Medicine considers a regular exercise program to be essential for most adults. It endorses one that includes cardiorespiratory, resistance, flexibility, and neuromotor exercise training, beyond the usual activities of daily living, to improve and maintain physical fitness and health. It is recommended that you do a combination of *aerobic* activities that increase your heart rate and breathing (see the Examples of Aerobic Exercise Intensity table below), *strength* activities that build and maintain bones and muscle, and *balance and stretching* activities that increase physical stability and flexibility, such as yoga, tai chi, or just basic stretches.

When you do aerobic exercise, your body's large muscles (such as your quadriceps or hamstring muscles in your legs) move for a sustained period, your heart rate and breathing rate increase, and you get sweaty. Three components of aerobic exercise influence the amount of benefit you get from each workout:

1. Intensity—how hard you work (described as moderate or vigorous intensity)
2. Frequency—how often you do the activity (once or twice a week, for example)
3. Duration—how long you do the activity (10 minutes? half an hour?)

Strength activities are those that cause the body's muscles to work against a force, such as when you pick up a weight or press against a resistance band. This is also called resistance exercise. Muscle-strengthening activities also have three components that influence the amount of benefit you derive from the exercise:

1. Intensity—how much weight is used (how heavy a weight you lift in pounds)
2. Frequency—how often you do the activity
3. Repetitions—how many times you lift the weight or repeat the motion

Intensity and Duration of Physical Activity

The recommended exercise guidelines for healthy adults are

- at least 30 minutes of moderate activity 5 times a week and 2 or more days of strength training each week

or

- at least 25 minutes of vigorous activity 3 times a week and 2 or more days of strength training each week

Examples of Aerobic Exercise Intensity

Moderate Intensity Activity	*Vigorous Intensity Activity*
Walk (3.5 mph)	Walk fast (4 to 4.5 mph)
Water aerobics	Jog, run (>5.0 mph)
Bike on level ground	Swim laps
Tennis—doubles	Aerobics class
Mow the lawn	Aerobic equipment (elliptical trainer, etc.)
Clean the house	Bike fast or up hills, or spinning class
Dance	Tennis—singles
Canoe, Kayak	Basketball
Golf	Soccer
Garden	Heavy gardening
Baseball, softball	Hiking uphill
Play with children	Jump rope

Sources: U.S. Department of Health and Human Services, 2008 Physical Activity Guidelines for Americans, www.health.gov/paguidelines, accessed April 2012; Centers for Disease Control and Prevention, "Measuring Physical Activity Intensity," www.cdc.gov/physicalactivity/everyone/measuring, accessed April 2012.

What is considered moderate or vigorous activity? The intensity depends on how much effort you are putting into it. To estimate the intensity of your physical activity, use the Talking Test. If you are able to talk while exercising, that is a *moderate* activity. If you are out of breath, that is a *vigorous* activity.

Or you could count your heart rate during exercise to determine whether you are exercising at a moderate or vigorous intensity. Do this by placing two fingers on the side of your neck or on the inside of your wrist and count the beats for one minute. Take this number and compare it to the percentage of your target heart rate.

- Your target heart rate is 220 minus your age.
- Exercising at 50 to 60 percent of your target HR is moderate intensity exercise.

- Exercising at 70 to 85 percent of your target HR is vigorous intensity exercise.

Track Your Progress

As you keep up your exercise program, your strength, endurance, and energy level will improve. The more you do, the stronger you will become, and the more likely you are to do the activity. Tracking your progress is a good way to monitor your activities, adjust your exercise as you improve, and keep up your motivation. One way to do this is to record the type and duration of your physical activities in a weekly agenda or exercise log. Another way is to use the USDA's online tool, Super Tracker (www.choosemyplate.gov/SuperTracker/physicalactivitytracker.aspx), which offers a way to track your exercise and your calories over time.

Routine and Structure

Routine and consistency in daily life help make your life more manageable and in control. It is thought that small changes in one's daily routine place stress on the body's ability to maintain stability, and that those with mood disorders have a more difficult time adapting to these changes in routine. Paying close attention to daily routines, and to the positive and negative events that influence those routines and cause you stress, increases your stability. This is the basis of social rhythm therapy, a treatment for bipolar disorder, which has some benefit to mood disorders in general.

Many people with depression have a difficult time going about their daily activities. However, endless hours of empty time alone will only worsen your symptoms. So it is essential to maintain a regular routine and structure to each day, even when you don't feel like it. Schedule your time and try to follow that schedule, but also be flexible with yourself. Keep your schedule in an agenda or appointment book that you carry with you. Having a daily structure and following a routine will also help you better manage the lack of interest and decreased energy that often comes with depression.

Plan your time each day to include a *balance* of these things:

- Responsibilities and obligations: things you do at work, home, school, with family
- Daily self-care
  - Meals and nutrition
  - Medications, treatments, therapy
  - Personal care: showering, shaving, brushing your teeth, getting dressed
  - Sleep
  - Exercise
- Social contacts: keep regular contact with safe people and situations. Avoid isolation. Being with people you like has a positive effect on your mood.
- Positive experiences
  - Pleasant and pleasurable activities: It is not enough to eliminate the negative experiences in life—you also need to include positive and pleasurable experiences.
  - Mastery activities: Engage in activities that are somewhat difficult for you to do and are a challenge. They give a sense of being competent and effective. Learning a new skill or overcoming an obstacle is one way to achieve mastery.
  - Purpose in life: include activities that give you a sense of purpose.

Keep your daily schedule . . .

- Prioritized. Understand what is most important for you to do.
- Measurable. Put a timeframe around each activity (instead of open-ended time).
- Attainable and realistic. Start with the things that you can do *now*, in your current state.
  - Pace yourself.
  - Break large, complex tasks down into small steps that are more realistic and manageable.

  - Don't overschedule—this creates more stress and the potential for failure.
  - Learn to set limits and say "no" when you are overextended.
- Concrete and specific. Clearly define each goal and task.
- Flexible. Understand where you are and what you can do at any given time and modify your schedule as needed. Do not compare your current self and abilities to past levels of performance or functioning.

To make it easier to include them in your daily structure, list activities, exercise, and people you enjoy (see form on page 27).

Avoiding Isolation

With depression, there is a tendency to withdraw from the activities of your daily life and to avoid contact with friends and family. You may prefer to stay at home, not get dressed or answer the telephone, and just do nothing. Getting in touch with others or responding to those who are trying to help you is often quite difficult. Symptoms of depression such as fatigue and lack of interest may contribute to your withdrawal. This type of alone time is often lonely, closed off, and adds to your sense of sadness. Resist the urge to isolate and withdraw from your life. Isolation is not healthy for you or your brain. Social isolation and lack of social support increase the risk of developing depression and may prolong episodes of depression. You need to have social contact and support to maintain your emotional well-being and protect against major depression.

Examples of isolation and withdrawal include:

- Staying alone at home most of the time, without others around
- Avoiding conversations with your family or friends, in person or by not making or returning telephone calls
- Not going out to be with other people
- Skipping your usual errands and human interactions

ACTIVITIES AND PEOPLE I ENJOY

Things I like (or used to like) to do:

Types of physical exercise I like (or used to like)—
only those things I can do now:

People I like to keep in contact with:

- Avoiding activities you once enjoyed
- Canceling plans with others for no particular reason
- Not making new plans
- Canceling doctor's appointments

Isolation versus Solitude

All alone time is not the same. Spending *some* time alone each day, without feeling lonely, can be beneficial. Solitude, rather than isolation, has a purpose and provides a sense of contentment and enjoyment. It allows you to think, self-reflect, and relax or replenish yourself when overwhelmed. Solitude is something you choose to experience, in contrast to the isolation of depression. Everyone needs a bit of alone time in their lives. A quiet walk outdoors, reading, or working on a favorite hobby are examples of solitude that can be valuable to your well-being. Even though solitude is alone time, it is not the same as the isolation and withdrawal that comes with depression.

People vary in how much they value and feel comfortable being alone. That is built into your disposition, the way you were born, and each person is different. You have to know yourself and your personal preferences. For example, a farmer tending to his cattle or crops all day or a fisherman at sea may feel quite content and not lonely or isolated, even though he does not see other people for days at a time. He is not bothered by being alone in his chosen place. This may be a healthy decision for him. Another person may not feel the same way and needs to be surrounded by others, such as by living in a large metropolitan city. People choose lifestyles with varying degrees of solitude, based on what is healthy for them.

How Do You Avoid Isolation and Withdrawal?

The first step is to recognize when it is happening. If you notice yourself spending more time alone, not by choice but because you are fatigued and have no interest or energy, this is isolation. If you find yourself avoiding people and activities for no particular reason, this is withdrawal. Know the signs of isolation for you and include these on your Action Plan for Relapse Prevention (see chapter 5).

Once you have identified your alone time as isolation and withdrawal, take steps to prevent it. Avoiding isolation when depressed can be a challenge. Do not wait until you "feel like it" to get out and be with others. Push yourself a little and just do it, a little bit at a time. Make it a point to return telephone calls from friends and family who are helpful and positive. Set your expectations to do the activities you can do now and modify them as needed. It can be overwhelming to do everything you managed when well, so break your activities down into small steps. Get out of the house. Do one or two errands at a time, not a dozen. Say hello to the store clerk. For now, walk for ten minutes around the block rather than tackling your usual exercise routine. Eventually, it will all become easier to do.

A written routine and schedule can help you manage the tendency to withdraw. That way, you have something concrete to follow for the times when you are so tempted to isolate. The key is to stick to your schedule even when you don't feel like it. Hold yourself accountable for following through. Then give yourself credit for this accomplishment!

DAILY SCHEDULE

Date	Monday	Tuesday	Wednesday
awake @			
7			
8			
9			
10			
11			
12			
1			
2			
3			
4			
5			
6			
7			
8			
9			
bedtime @			

Thursday	Friday	Saturday	Sunday

CHAPTER 2

Mood Disorders

Depression and Bipolar Disorder

Mood disorders is a term that includes major depression and bipolar disorder, conditions of the brain that involve a disturbance in your mood or state of mind. These two conditions are grouped together because they share some of the same clinical characteristics.

Major Depression

Major depression is most often a relapsing and remitting yet treatable illness. A relapsing and remitting condition means that the symptoms come and go. Depression affects your thoughts, feelings, behaviors, relationships, activities, interests, and many other aspects of life. Someone with depression often has trouble functioning in the ordinary activities of daily living. An episode of depression may last weeks, months, or longer. Many people have repeat episodes over time and feel well in between—the pattern is unique to each person.

One way to see patterns in your illness and its relationship to life events is to track your daily symptoms on a Mood Chart (page 46). Tracking these details is a good way to follow your progress and response to treatment. This information can then be used in making treatment decisions with your physician or as a point of discussion in psychotherapy sessions.

One long-held theory of depression is that it involves an imbalance of chemicals in the brain, called neurotransmitters. These chemicals are found throughout the brain, including the part that regulates your emotions and behavior. The chemical imbalance may happen when certain life experiences occur in a susceptible person. What makes a person susceptible is not fully understood.

A newer theory of depression is that the interaction of your genes with your environment and life experiences shapes the complex network of cells in your brain (called neurons). This shaping is thought to work in this way. The brain is sensitive to stressful and traumatic events during vulnerable periods in your life. Negative stimulation, such as stress or illness, changes the action of certain genes. This altered gene activity, in turn, affects the normal functioning of your brain. In summary, negative stimulation changes gene activity which results in dysfunction of the neural network in your brain. When that happens during a vulnerable period, the brain does not work well, and the result is depression.

Depression often runs in families, which supports the idea of a genetic basis for the illness. You may have genetic factors that make you more likely to suffer from depression, but this does not guarantee that you will have the illness. If you are genetically prone to depression, you may not have an episode unless you also experience certain stressful life events. These experiences are thought to affect the genes that regulate your brain functioning. Examples of stressful life events include major trauma (a major loss or death), chronic stress, hormonal changes (such as during peri-menopause or postpartum), medical illness, substance abuse, sleep disorders, and others. Depression is not entirely genetic, and it is not entirely related to life experiences.

The symptoms of depression are psychological, behavioral, and physical. Major depression is characterized by feeling sad or depressed with loss of interest in activities. According to the standard diagnostic manual of psychiatric disorders (the DSM-IV-TR), to be diagnosed with major depression, you must have at least five of the following symptoms, lasting for two weeks or more:

- sad, depressed, or irritable feelings most of the day
- loss of interest or pleasure in most activities
- sleep changes—too much, too little, or with early morning awakening
- weight loss or gain (without trying)

- loss of energy
- decreased ability to think or concentrate
- restlessness or the sensation of being physically slowed down
- thoughts of worthlessness, hopelessness, guilt
- thoughts of death and suicide

An updated version of the diagnostic manual, the DSM-5, is scheduled for publication in the spring of 2013. The symptoms required to diagnose depression are expected to remain constant. For an in-depth discussion of these symptoms of depression, see Beck and Alford, *Depression: Causes and Treatment.*

What does an episode of depression feel like? Living with it is very hard on you and your family and friends. Depression is not just "feeling blue" for a day. It is far beyond sadness. With depression comes deep despair, physical and emotional pain, and suffering. There is often a near paralysis, being unable to participate in and enjoy life, physically and mentally. With depression, the world is gray and murky and you see only the negative side of life. You may feel guilty, worthless, and without hope. Irritability may be your main response to the world around you. You lose interest in the things you used to like and may not experience any pleasure. Motivation is nearly gone. Sleep may not come, or there may be too much of it, yet it is hard to get out of bed and move about. Fatigue is overwhelming. Food has no taste. You withdraw from people and activities and may lose friends. Communication and small talk is a major effort. Your thinking slows down, and it is hard to concentrate and focus. School and work suffer. Projects and assignments and the mail pile up, and you may spend hours just staring, unable to approach the task at hand. The thoughts you have are often distorted and negative, yet they seem quite believable to you. Your thinking may be quite disorganized. And at times, you may believe that death will bring relief.

Bipolar Disorder

Bipolar disorder, which used to be called manic-depressive disorder, is also a relapsing and remitting mood disorder that significantly affects daily life. As with major depression, it is thought to be caused by a dysfunction in the network of neurons in the brain. Bipolar disorder is characterized by periodic episodes of extreme elevated mood or irritability followed by periodic episodes of depression. These episodes come in cycles, in a different pattern for each person. In bipolar disorder, many people spend more of their illness time in the depressed phase rather than the elevated (manic) phase of the disorder. The symptoms of bipolar depression are similar to those of major depression.

To be diagnosed with a manic episode, according to the DSM-IV-TR, you need to have experienced an elevated or irritable mood that impairs your functioning for at least one week as well as three or more of the following symptoms:

- inflated sense of self or grandiosity
- increased physical and mental activity and energized or psychomotor agitation
- decreased need for sleep
- racing thoughts
- distractibility, poor concentration
- pressured speech, which means a certain way of being more talkative than usual
- irritability
- high-risk behavior (such as excessive spending, impulsive sexual behavior, and so on)

There are different types of bipolar disorder that span a spectrum of these symptoms. The type depends on the intensity and duration of the elevated mood symptoms. A manic episode is as described above, hypomanic episodes are shorter and less intense, and mixed episodes are a combination of depression and mania or hypomania that occur at the same time.

What does bipolar disorder feel like? Living through the different phases of depressed, manic, hypomanic or mixed episodes is very hard. When depressed, you may withdraw from friends and family or feel too irritable to be with people. You may often be unable to concentrate and function well at work or school. Being manic or hypomanic is like having a storm inside your head. Your thoughts and speech race from topic to topic without completing a thought. You may be too disorganized and distracted to function well without realizing it at the time. In fact, when manic, you might think that you can do anything you choose, and that you have great ideas. You may start and stop multiple projects without finishing any of them. You feel a minimal need for sleep, yet you feel energized, not tired. You may have extreme impulses and may engage in high-risk activities, such as exorbitant shopping, excessive sexual behaviors, or driving too fast. Your impulses may lead to making poor financial or business decisions. All of this has an effect on your life and in your relationships with friends, family, and work colleagues.

Depression in Women

Some women's depression symptoms worsen in relation to changes in their female hormones: estrogen and progesterone. This may happen at certain points in the menstrual cycle or at other times when hormone levels fluctuate, such as during the transition to menopause (peri-menopause) or after the birth of a child (postpartum). The relationship between mood and hormones is not well understood, but research is progressing. A valuable resource where you can learn more about current thinking and research on psychiatric issues throughout a woman's reproductive life is the Web site www.womensmentalhealth.org. There you will find a library of information, a blog, and a newsletter of up-to-date topics on depression and PMS, peri-natal and postpartum depression, fertility and mental health, and menopausal symptoms.

To find a potential association between hormone levels and your depression, use the Mood Chart on page 46 to track your moods.

Make sure that you include the days of your menstrual cycle and other important dates on the chart, such as the birth of a child or your last menstrual period. Then share the completed chart with your doctor.

Depression and Anxiety

Approximately half of those who suffer from depression also suffer from anxiety at the same time. This adds a great burden to the weight of feeling depressed. Anxiety is a condition where you feel excessive apprehension, nervousness, and worry about several events or activities. It is often accompanied by feeling restless or shaky, with difficulty concentrating, irritability, and disturbed sleep. The intensity, duration, and frequency of the anxiety or worry is out of proportion to the actual feared event and causes distress. The fear feels very real and scary at the time. You may feel nervous, jittery, worried, and sweaty, with your heart racing or skipping a beat, an upset stomach, and muscle aches. People experiencing severe anxiety symptoms often go to the Emergency Department for fear that something physical is wrong. The good news is that many treatments for mood disorders, including those mentioned in this book, are also effective for treating anxiety.

The Stigma of Mood Disorders

Mood disorders such as depression and bipolar disorder still carry a stigma, even in the year 2012. A stigma arises when some people judge you because of your illness and then label you with a negative stereotype or image. Some people believe that it is socially unacceptable to have a mood disorder. They may try to make you feel ashamed or disgraced because of your illness. Some people may believe you are incompetent, potentially dangerous, weak in character, or undesirable just because of your illness. They will be judgmental and critical of you. *But they are mistaken! Their beliefs are absolutely not true!*

There is nothing unacceptable about having a biologically based condition such as depression or bipolar disorder (or diabetes or heart disease, for that matter). Unfortunately, many people are not informed about mood disorders as an illness, and they believe in the stigma. They may try to force their inaccurate beliefs and attitudes on you. Ill-informed beliefs and judgments may come from your friends, family, or strangers who just don't know any better. Remember that their misinformation is driving this behavior—it is not a reflection of you.

Having an illness with a stigma attached is an additional burden for you to carry on top of the depression symptoms you already feel. Having to deal with others' inaccurate reactions to and criticism of your illness can magnify the suffering you experience. You may feel you are constantly choosing whether to feel hurt, and deal with that, or correct their misinformation, if you feel you have the mental energy to do so. When others attach a stigma to your illness, it can put a strain on your relationship with them at home, at work, or in social situations. Often, you need to step back and understand that you may never be able to turn around the other person's thinking no matter how hard you try. Consider what you know about the person—the source of their distorted beliefs—and try to ignore the comments of those whose opinion you cannot change.

Fatigue and Depression

Fatigue is a common symptom that affects people in both the general community and medical care settings, including psychiatry. It is considered to be a core symptom in mood disorders, affecting more than 75 percent of patients with major depression. Fatigue can significantly impair your ability to function and carry out your daily tasks. It may make it more difficult to get up and out of bed, get dressed, care for yourself or your family, prepare meals, or get out of the house to do errands or go to work. You may feel fatigue even when you think you are getting enough sleep, which can be quite frustrating.

What exactly is fatigue? There is no single definition. It is different from just feeling sleepy or tired. Fatigue can be thought of as a combination of symptoms, with three main dimensions: physical, mental, and emotional. You may have several of these together. The multiple components of fatigue have been described in this way:

Physical

- loss of energy
- heavy limbs
- persistent tiredness even without physical exertion
- exhaustion
- reduced activity tolerance
- decreased physical endurance, stamina
- increased effort required to accomplish physical tasks
- generalized weakness
- slowness or sluggishness

Mental and cognitive

- mental dulling
- word finding and recall problems
- problems focusing and sustaining attention
- difficulty concentrating
- decreased mental endurance
- slowed thinking

Emotional and psychological

- lack of motivation
- apathy, decreased interest
- weariness
- irritability
- boredom
- low mood

The various dimensions of fatigue are included in the DSM-IV-TR definition of depression, for example, physical fatigue (loss of energy), mental fatigue (difficulty concentrating), and emotional fatigue (loss of interest and pleasure, called *anhedonia*).

Depression-related fatigue has various possible causes, which may be difficult to sort out. But it is important to identify which one applies to you, if possible, so that you and your provider can address and treat the problem of fatigue effectively.

First, fatigue may be a *primary symptom* of your depression, along with other feelings of low mood, sadness, or loss of interest. Often the fatigue improves along with the treatment for depression. However, fatigue can also be a *residual symptom* of depression, persisting after treatment in 22.5 to 38 percent of people who are otherwise in remission. This means that, in some people, fatigue persists even after most other depression symptoms have improved or gone away following treatment with antidepressant medication. Residual fatigue can be difficult to resolve, but therapeutic options are available—speak with your psychiatrist if you are having persistent fatigue.

Next, fatigue can be a *side effect* of antidepressant medications, particularly some SSRIs (selective serotonin reuptake inhibitors). Sometimes this requires a change in medication to a different drug with fewer side effects, one that you tolerate better. This requires a discussion with your treating psychiatrist. Remember to be specific about your side effect symptoms and how they affect the quality of your life.

Fatigue can also be *related to insomnia* and poor sleep patterns, which often occur along with depression. If this is a cause of your fatigue, adhering to good Sleep Hygiene practices will benefit you. Finally, fatigue may be *related to other medical problems* you may have. These problems may include diabetes; low thyroid condition; kidney, liver, lung, or heart disease; and others. These conditions do not necessarily cause the fatigue; there is just a potential association. In these cases, work with your treating physician to optimize your other medical conditions as best as possible.

What Helps with Fatigue?

Begin by investigating the conditions that may be contributing to your fatigue and work with your treatment team to modify what you can. You may need to avoid those antidepressant medications that are likely to worsen sleepiness and fatigue, choose antidepressant medications more likely to help resolve the symptoms, and consider using an additional medication that targets fatigue. Discuss these options with your psychiatrist.

Next, stick to the Basics of Mental Health covered in the first chapter of this book. Remember to have regular nutritious meals, follow a regular sleeping and waking pattern (with a goal of getting 8 hours sleep per night), take your medications as prescribed, avoid alcohol and illegal substances, maintain a daily routine and schedule, and keep up with social contacts. Then, even though it sounds difficult, get out and exercise a little every day, at a moderate level, based on your current ability. Yes, even when fatigued! You will be surprised how much exercise will improve your energy level.

Symptoms of Depression

Depression affects your thoughts, feelings, and behaviors, which can interfere with the quality of your life. The most common symptoms include a deep feeling of sadness, loss of interest and pleasure in your usual activities; changes in appetite, weight, and sleep; loss of energy; fatigue; irritability; feelings of worthlessness, hopelessness, and guilt; difficulty thinking, concentrating, and making decisions; and thoughts of suicide.

The form on page 43 provides examples of common thoughts, feelings, and behaviors related to depression. Check off those you can relate to and share this information with your treatment team.

Symptoms of Elevated Mood

The extremely elevated mood of bipolar disorder affects your thoughts, feelings, and behaviors, which can interfere with the quality of your life. The form on page 44 provides examples of common thoughts, feelings, and behaviors related to elevated mood. Check off those you can relate to and share this information with your treatment team.

SYMPTOMS OF DEPRESSION

NEGATIVE THOUGHTS

__ I deserve this.
__ I am being punished.
__ It's all my fault.
__ I can't make decisions.
__ I can't remember anything.
__ Nothing good will ever happen.
__ Things will never get better.
__ I never do anything right.
__ I am not as good as everyone else.
__ Nobody will ever care about me.
__ I am worthless.
__ People are against me.
__ I should do/be ______________.
__ I have wasted my (life, education, opportunities).
__ There is no hope for me.
__ I think about dying or suicide a lot.

FEELINGS

__ I feel sad for no reason.
__ I don't feel good even if good things happen.
__ I feel worthless.
__ I feel bad, inferior to other people.
__ I feel guilty about everything.
__ I feel easily annoyed or irritable.
__ I fear that something terrible will happen.
__ I feel tired all the time.
__ I am not interested in anything.
__ I am not interested in sex.

BEHAVIORS

__ I cry a lot for no reason.
__ I sleep too much.
__ I sleep too little.
__ I eat too much.
__ I eat very little.
__ I drink too much alcohol.
__ I recently gained a lot of weight.
__ I recently lost a lot of weight without trying.
__ I stay in bed or on the couch all day.
__ Sometimes I don't take a shower, wash my hair, or shave.
__ I have trouble starting or finishing projects.
__ I avoid people and isolate myself.
__ I do not return telephone calls.
__ I have stopped my previous activities, hobbies.
__ I stopped exercising.
__ I argue and fight with people for no good reason.
__ I am fidgety and restless.
__ I move or speak slowly.
__ I have trouble concentrating.
__ I have difficulty reading the newspaper or following shows on TV.
__ I can't keep track of my thoughts well enough to have a conversation.
__ My house is more disorganized than usual.
__ I forget to pay bills.
__ I forget or don't do laundry or other household duties.
__ I call in sick to work or school a lot.

SYMPTOMS OF ELEVATED MOOD

ELEVATED THOUGHTS

__ I have special abilities.
__ I have a lot of good ideas.
__ My thoughts are really great.
__ Many people are interested in me and my ideas.
__ Many people are against me.
__ I get very focused on a project or cause.
__ My thoughts jump around quickly from one topic to another.
__ Other people say they can't follow what I'm saying.
__ The rest of the world is too slow.
__ It takes others a really long time to do things.

FEELINGS

__ I feel good even when bad things happen.
__ I feel happy without reason.
__ I am very self-confident.
__ I have lots of energy even when I get less sleep than usual.
__ I feel optimistic about everything.
__ I feel great, on top of the world.
__ I feel that everything will go my way.
__ I feel that nothing bad can happen to me.
__ I am easily annoyed or irritable.
__ I am very impatient.
__ I feel more interested in sex than usual.

BEHAVIORS

__ I sleep less than usual and don't feel tired.
__ I laugh a lot or for no reason.
__ I am more talkative than usual.
__ I am fidgety and restless, and I pace a lot.
__ I have trouble concentrating.
__ I am easily distracted.
__ I start lots of new projects and activities.
__ I have increased my activities, work, hobbies.
__ I don't finish projects before starting new ones.
__ I am much more sociable than usual.
__ I make more phone calls than usual.
__ I spend money, go on shopping sprees.
__ I make impulsive decisions.
__ I tip excessively, gamble.
__ I take more risks than usual.
__ I do more risky or dangerous activities.
__ I start arguments or fights for no reason.
__ I drive fast.
__ I increase my use of alcohol or drugs.
__ I dress more flashy than usual.
__ My handwriting is larger and messier.

Mood Chart

Use the chart on page 46 to record your mood every day, then share it with your provider. Check the box that best estimates your mood for that day, such as a depressed or elevated mood that is severe, moderate, or mild in intensity. Doing this will help you track fluctuations or identify a pattern in your moods. Use the Notes column to record anything that might have affected your mood—stressful events, medication changes, or (in women) your menstrual period.

MOOD CHART

Month:

Day	Depressed			Neutral	Elevated Mood			Notes
	mild	*moderate*	*severe*		*mild*	*moderate*	*severe*	
1								
2								
3								
4								
5								
6								
7								
8								
9								
10								
11								
12								
13								
14								
15								
16								
17								
18								
19								
20								
21								
22								
23								
24								
25								
26								
27								
28								
29								
30								
31								

CHAPTER 3

Defining Your Baseline

What Is Your Baseline?

With depression, you may have difficulty remembering what you were like before the episode. You may often struggle to differentiate the symptoms of depression from "just me, my regular self." Depression can take away your sense of who you are as a human being (your inner sense of self). It feels like there is nothing *but* depression in life. You forget what you are like, or used to be like, and you may not feel familiar to yourself. You may forget what your basic competencies are, your baseline skills and accomplishments. In managing depression, you have to *find a way to stay connected to your inner sense of self,* to your baseline person. Having your baseline healthy self to draw on is an important aid during your recovery. This will help you envision what you are working toward. *You* are not your depression.

How do you do that?

One way is with the following exercise . . .

Step 1

Create a list of your strengths and weaknesses, personal preferences, beliefs, values, skills, and competencies. Be realistic when you assess your strengths and weaknesses.

Include your personal preferences, your likes and dislikes, needs, wants, skills, values, beliefs, opinions, sense of purpose, what nourishes you, energizes you, gives you pleasure and enjoyment, a sense of perspective and calm. Identify what makes life rich and full for you.

STRENGTHS AND WEAKNESSES

This exercise is one of several steps to help you connect with your sense of self. In each column below, list your personal strengths and weaknesses. Be honest with yourself. Get feedback from others who know you well if you have difficulty doing this exercise.

MY STRENGTHS	MY WEAKNESSES

CHAPTER 4

Managing Your Mood Disorder

Following Your Treatment Plan

Treating your depression and bipolar disorder is ideally a collaborative effort between you and your doctor(s) that often includes both medication and talk therapy, also called psychotherapy. Most people seek treatment to feel better and to function better. Treatment can also help you learn new skills, understand and manage your emotions, and deal with difficulties in your relationships.

Most people with depression or bipolar disorder are treated in an outpatient (office) setting. Usually, a psychiatrist is the doctor who prescribes medication and works with you to create an overall treatment plan. In some cases, an internist or a family doctor prescribes the medication. Depression is most often treated with an antidepressant. Bipolar disorder may be treated with mood-stabilizing medications, such as lithium or others. It may take 6 to 8 weeks after starting a medication for you to begin to see improvement. You may have to try several different ones before finding the most effective medication or combination of medications for you.

It is essential to stay on the medication once your symptoms have started to improve. Stopping it too soon puts you at risk for recurrence (return) of your symptoms. This does not mean that you are dependent on the drug. Unfortunately, research has shown that non-adherence (not sticking) with antidepressant medication is a common problem, with only half of patients continuing an adequate dose of therapy in the short term. Those patients are at risk for not getting better or for having their symptoms return. This is why it is important to continue to see your physician, preferably a psychiatric specialist, on a regular basis until your symptoms clear.

Psychotherapy (talk therapy) is a significant treatment for mood disorders, and alone or combined with medication, it has been effective in preventing further episodes of depression. It is a type of guided therapeutic conversation that focuses on your psychological and emotional problems, distorted thinking, and troublesome behaviors. The mental health professional who specializes in talk therapy is usually a clinical psychologist, who will work with you to create a psychotherapy treatment plan. The success of psychotherapy depends on building a trusting relationship with a therapist who is a good fit for you. Psychotherapy takes time and effort to see results. It is not a passive treatment—you need to do a lot of hard work to gain from it. Sometimes you benefit from the work you do during appointments (individual or group therapy). Often the benefits come from work you do during the rest of the week, when you have the opportunity to apply to your daily life what you have learned in your sessions. Treatment often involves making some change in the way you think or behave, and that may be uncomfortable. Changing to something unfamiliar can be both scary and hopeful. It is scary because you are doing something different and perhaps a little uncomfortable, and hopeful because the purpose is to feel better. Psychotherapy may also stir up unpleasant emotions. Dealing with these emotions is important to your recovery.

There are many different types of psychotherapy, each with a different name. The type you receive depends on your problems and your needs. Cognitive behavioral therapy (CBT) is a form of talk therapy that has been extensively tested and shown to be very effective in treating depression and reducing the risk of relapse (return of symptoms). Mindfulness-based CBT is a somewhat different approach that is also effective for some people. Another type of psychotherapy, dialectical behavior therapy (DBT), teaches concrete cognitive behavioral and mindfulness skills in four modules: mindfulness, interpersonal effectiveness, emotion regulation, and distress tolerance. It has been shown to be an effective augmentation (additional) therapy to antidepressant medication, resulting in improvement in depression symptoms.

Medication therapy and psychotherapy alone are each effective in treating depression and reducing the risk of relapse and recurrence. In combination, they offer an even greater benefit against relapse. They are seen as therapies that complement each other. Psychotherapy offers a broader range of benefits, such as improving your level of functioning, diminishing residual symptoms, targeting specific symptoms (such as guilt, hopelessness, and pessimism), teaching coping skills, improving interpersonal relationships, and targeting different brain sites than antidepressants do. The effects of psychotherapy are longer lasting and sustained beyond the end of treatment.

Sometimes the symptoms of your mood disorder worsen to the point where treatment in an inpatient hospital setting is needed. Inpatient care is a more intense form of treatment, where you receive daily individual and group therapy as well as medication management. Entering the hospital can be a scary experience the first time you are admitted, especially when you do not feel well and do not know what to expect. It can also be difficult if you do not feel the support of family or friends, who may not understand your illness or its treatment. However, an inpatient unit provides a safe environment during a rough time. This is especially important for those who have disorganized or suicidal thoughts. Most people treated in a hospital find it to be extremely helpful and even lifesaving.

On the inpatient unit, you work with a team of mental health professionals who review your current treatment plan and may suggest modifications. The inpatient team usually includes a senior psychiatrist, psychologist, nurse, social worker, and sometimes an occupational therapist. A teaching hospital will also have psychiatry residents, medical students, and sometimes nursing students. Your inpatient treatment plan is a collaborative plan between you and your team; you have the right to decide what feels appropriate and helpful for you, as long as it is safe. In some cases, treatments such as ECT (electroconvulsive therapy, also called shock therapy) may be recommended as part of your plan. You will also receive the support and input of other patients in group therapy sessions.

In addition to taking medications and participating in psychotherapy, taking steps to manage your illness in your everyday life is essential. Helping yourself in this way offers the best chance of recovery and of staying well. You can learn to manage your illness in this and the next few chapters.

The Relationship with Your Therapist

The success of your treatment, particularly psychotherapy, depends on building a trusting relationship with a therapist who is a good fit for you. How do you find this therapist? That answer varies among individuals. One place to start is to ask your psychiatrist or primary care doctor for a recommendation. Depending on who is available in your geographic area, he or she may refer you to a clinical psychologist, licensed therapist, or licensed clinical social worker. Try to find one who specializes in treating patients with depression. If you live near a large teaching hospital, most academic Psychiatry Departments have a specialized Depression Unit that can refer you to a staff member. Get several names and then interview each one *face to face* to see if you feel comfortable speaking with this person. Not everyone will be a good match for you, so keep looking until you find someone you think will work. Do not be afraid to ask questions of the people you interview. Inquire about their training and background. Find out if they can schedule your appointments around your work hours. Ask about the method of payment and whether or not your health insurance company will pay for it. Make sure that the person you choose will coordinate your care with your other doctors (psychiatrist, family doctor, etc.).

What Makes a Good Therapist?

There are many different therapists, each with a particular style, personality, and training. They may also practice different types of psychotherapy. Those differences do not prevent them from delivering good quality care.

You should expect that a good therapist

- listens and pays attention
- is empathetic and understanding
- is not judgmental or dismissive
- shows respect
- builds trust over time
- offers sound professional advice
- maintains boundaries
- does not impose his or her personal biases or viewpoints on you
- helps you to see your way through a problem and does not do it for you
- builds on your strengths
- offers you a regular appointment at the same time and day
- begins and ends appointments on time
- does not take telephone calls or allow other distractions during your appointment
- is available to you by page or telephone after hours for emergencies
- maintains your privacy and confidentiality

What Makes a Good Patient?

What do you need to do to get the most benefit from your therapy? Show by your actions that you are interested in and committed to talk therapy. Participating in therapy is a two-way street, and you have to do a lot of the work. You also need to keep up a good professional relationship with your therapist. Helping yourself in this way provides the best chance of recovery and of staying well.

These guidelines will help you be successful in therapy:

- Follow all treatments as prescribed. This includes taking medications and acting on other recommended therapies.
- Keep your appointments as scheduled. Do not skip appointments or cancel them at the last minute unless there is an emergency.
- Go to your appointments on time and stay for the entire session.
- Arrive sober. Do not show up to your appointment under the influence of alcohol or drugs.
- Be honest with your therapist.
- Make an effort.
- Do the "homework" assignments that your therapist asks you to do.
- Come prepared for each session with an idea of what you would like to discuss or work on with your therapist.
- Turn off your cell phone, iPad, and other electronic devices during your appointment.
- Listen.
- Pay attention to the conversation. Catch yourself if you begin to daydream off the subject.
- Take notes if you are having trouble concentrating or remembering what is being discussed.
- Show respect.
- Maintain boundaries. This is a professional relationship, not a casual friendship.
- Control your anger and outbursts during the session. If anger is a problem for you, your therapist will make addressing it part of your treatment plan.
- Learn to trust the therapist and understand that he or she has your best interest in mind.
- Avoid making phone calls to your therapist unless the situation is urgent.
- Call your therapist or go to the nearest Emergency Department if you are feeling unsafe or suicidal.

Managing Depression and Bipolar Disorder

Managing your depression or bipolar disorder effectively is critical to maintaining your emotional balance and stability. It can help you feel and function better. People who participate actively in their care and work to manage their illness have a better chance of recovery and of staying well. Some people find that the symptoms of depression interfere with what they must do to manage their illness. For example, the symptoms of fatigue, poor appetite and sleep, and lack of interest can interfere with your ability to get the physical exercise necessary for a healthy life. This makes managing your illness a challenge, but it can be done. And it will make a difference.

What does it mean to manage your illness? It means that you learn about the illness and that you use certain methods, strategies, and skills each day to respond to the symptoms you have. These strategies are discussed in detail in this chapter. Developing the tools to deal with your illness will help you recover, prevent worsening, and avoid relapse (a return of symptoms).

Managing your depression effectively requires that you pay attention to your symptoms and monitor them, challenge negative thoughts, use problem-solving techniques, make adjustments, and avoid negative behaviors (see chapter 5). It means that you regulate your daily routine and make efforts to improve current relationships. Effective management also includes attending to self-care, following a healthy lifestyle and diet, getting physical exercise, and following the treatment plan you developed with your provider.

Self-management is best done in collaboration with your health care provider(s), who work with you and guide you along the way. You need to be partners in the process and participate in making decisions about treatment, interpreting and managing changes in your condition, coping with emotional reactions, implementing behavioral changes, and using medical and community resources wisely. Actively managing your illness may enable standard therapies to work better and may decrease the risk of relapse.

Managing Depression and Bipolar Disorder

Living with depression is a lot of hard work. For the best chance of success, you will need to take the following steps:

- Accept it as an illness.
- Follow your treatment plan.
- Understand the fluctuations (changes) in your symptoms and your symptom patterns.
- Define your baseline.
- Identify and monitor your Triggers (chapter 5).
- Identify and monitor your Early Warning Signs and Symptoms (chapter 5).
- Develop an Action Plan to use when things get worse, when you or others notice your Warning Signs (chapter 5).
- Use Relapse Prevention Strategies. Relapse Prevention is a day-to-day approach to help you stay well (chapter 5).
- Learn and use effective Coping Skills (chapter 7).
- Maintain social connections. Avoid isolation.
- Maintain self-care.
- Have a daily routine and structure. Schedule your time.
- Do something every day, even when you don't feel like it.
- Build mastery (chapters 5 and 6).
- Develop a tolerance for feeling distress for a short time, during a moment of crisis (chapter 7).

Research has shown an improvement in depression symptoms when patients collaborated with their providers, were educated about the illness, shared decision making about medications, and used cognitive behavioral strategies to promote self-management. These strategies included keeping track of depression symptoms, monitoring yourself for early Warning Signs, socializing, engaging in pleasant activities, and developing a written self-care plan for situations that could lead to a worsening or recurrence of depression. Another study showed the importance of these factors in helping people with mood disorders stick with taking their antidepressant medications, which contributes to better depression outcomes.

Managing your mood disorder involves the following steps (which are also listed in the Managing Depression and Bipolar Disorder table, on page 64).

Acceptance

Accept your depression or bipolar disorder as an illness, an illness that affects your body and your mind. It is not a weakness or character flaw, or something that you have complete control over. It is an illness that can be treated and managed in a way that minimizes the effect of the illness on the quality of your life. Sometimes family or friends have a different opinion about your mood disorder or try to help by offering suggestions that are unfortunately misinformed. Do not listen to these differing viewpoints.

Follow Your Treatment Plan

The treatment plan developed by your providers, with your input and approval, is designed to help you. Take all medications as prescribed, and notify your doctor if you take any over-the-counter or nonprescription drugs. Keep taking your medications even after your symptoms have started to improve, and do not change the dose. Avoid alcohol and street drugs, which will only worsen your symptoms. It is also important to actively participate in your therapy sessions, do your prescribed homework exercises, and do not skip appointments.

Understand Your Fluctuations

Fluctuations are changes in your symptoms over time. You *will* have fluctuations up and down at different times during this illness. Use the Mood Chart on page 46 to identify them. From looking at this chart and working with your therapist, learn to understand the fluctuations in your symptoms and the patterns that you have. When you are experiencing an episode of depression, remembering that things will change for the better is hard. Try to remind yourself of this during those dark times. Aim to minimize the depth, intensity, and duration of your symptoms by working with your therapist and using the suggestions in this book.

Define Your Baseline

With depression or bipolar disorder, you may have trouble remembering anything but your current mood state. Find a way to stay connected to your sense of who you are, your inner sense of self. Remembering your baseline self, or healthier state of mind, will help you keep each episode in context, and you will feel more in control of your life. You are not your depression.

Having a clear image of your baseline healthy self to draw on during your recovery will help you know what you are working toward. You may need to ask people who know you well to help you. Ask your friends or family to remind you honestly of your strengths and unique personal qualities, then write them down. Review that list periodically. See chapter 3 for an exercise on how to do this.

Identify and Monitor Your Triggers

Triggers are events or circumstances that may cause you distress and lead to an increase in your symptoms. Being aware of what can worsen your symptoms is crucial to avoiding relapse (see page 74). You may not be able to change the Trigger itself, but you can learn to modify how you respond to it so that you do not feel as much distress. Work with your therapist to identify, monitor, and modify your response to your Triggers.

Identify and Monitor Your Early Warning Signs and Symptoms

Warning Signs are distinct changes from your baseline that precede an episode of depression or mania (see page 75). Each person has a characteristic pattern of Warning Signs. These are changes in your thoughts, feelings, behaviors, routine, or self-care that are noticeable to you or others. Being aware of the changes that are Warning Signs for you will help you recognize the signs early. This will give you a chance to intervene and change the course of the depression or bipolar episode.

Symptoms that might be Warning Signs are those characteristic to depression or mania that last for two weeks or longer (see chapter 2). They may include changes in appetite, sleep, thinking, or concentration; loss of interest; sad, worthless, hopeless, or guilty feelings; negative or elevated thoughts or feelings; or behavior that is slowed down, irritable, restless, or overactive.

Develop an Action Plan

An intervention Action Plan for Relapse Prevention is a written self-care plan to help you deal with a worsening or a recurrence of depression. It outlines the steps you will take to manage, cope with, and distract from the intensity of a depression or manic episode. In your plan, you also list the people you will ask to help you: health care providers, family, and friends. Work with your therapist to develop an intervention Action Plan to use when things get worse, when you or others notice your Warning Signs or a change in your emotional state. Create your Action Plan now and have it ready to use before you have any intense symptoms. See page 78 for a sample Action Plan.

Use Relapse Prevention Strategies

Relapse Prevention is a day-to-day approach to help you stay well. It is a way for you to identify, monitor, and respond early to changes in your symptoms. The approach also involves daily preventive steps to strengthen your emotional resources. For more information on Relapse Prevention, see chapter 5. A Relapse Prevention Strategy includes five main steps that you and your treatment team will act on:

1. Identify in advance what your Warning Signs are.
2. Pay attention to your Warning Signs. Notice when changes from baseline begin to show.
3. Have an Action Plan prepared in advance and ready to use when your symptoms change.
4. Follow daily prevention steps to help you remain stable.
5. If you notice a change in your emotional health, follow your Action Plan. The plan will enable you to intervene early and modify or improve the course of the episode.

Use Coping Skills

Coping skills are the actions we take to lessen the effect of stressors and to get us through difficult times. These skills include problem solving, self-soothing, distraction, relaxation, humor, and managing the little things before they get too big. Learning and using effective coping skills are essential to managing your mood disorder. Coping skills are discussed in more detail in chapter 7.

Connect

Maintaining social connections can be difficult to do on your own, so enlist the help of friends and family to stay in touch with you. Being with people you like has a positive effect on your mood. Avoid isolation and withdrawal because they will only worsen your depression. Some people find help in support groups with people who share the same illness and concerns.

Maintain Self-Care

Get up, take a shower, shave, wash your hair, and brush your teeth. Every day. Get dressed in clean, nice clothes and avoid wearing sweat pants all day long. Get a haircut or a manicure without feeling guilty. It does not diminish the seriousness of your illness. These things may sound simple, but they require a lot of energy and are challenging to do when depressed. They may also be the last thing you are interested in. But taking good care of your body will help you feel better about yourself. Don't forget to give yourself credit for these accomplishments.

Have a Daily Routine and Structure

Having a daily routine and structure can help in many ways, such as helping you to avoid spending endless hours of empty alone time, which will only worsen your symptoms of depression (see page 24). It also gives you a purpose to your day, which will help improve your self-esteem. Schedule your time and try to follow it, but don't be too rigid with yourself. Many people with depression struggle with their daily activities. Following a written schedule helps you to see and stick to everything you need to do, which feels good and is a daily accomplishment.

Do Something Every Day

With depression, your motivation to do anything seems to disappear, especially with how difficult it all seems to be during an episode. You may not feel like doing anything, but try anyway—at least *one* thing. Action precedes motivation. Do something every day, even when you don't feel like it. Interest in doing it will come later.

Build Mastery

Mastery involves doing something that is difficult and that challenges you a little. This may be learning a new skill or hobby, or overcoming an obstacle. When you work on a Mastery activity, you will feel more competent and effective, and you will gain a sense of achievement (see pages 25, 102). Give yourself credit for trying.

Develop Distress Tolerance

Distress Tolerance strategies involve using skills to help you get through the crisis of a difficult moment. These skills include distracting yourself, soothing yourself, providing solace, and improving the moment itself (see page 113). In a crisis you may sometimes feel a sense of urgency or desire to act impulsively. This can interfere with your efforts to manage depression and remain stable. Working to develop your tolerance for distress over a short period can help you get through the rough moments.

CHAPTER 5

Relapse Prevention

Overview of Relapse Prevention

The symptoms of major depression and bipolar disorder often fluctuate, or change up and down over time. It is important to understand that you will have fluctuations as part of the illness. The frequency and pattern of these changes will vary with each person. One way to identify your patterns is to track your symptoms on a Mood Chart (page 45) each day and share it with your physician.

At some point following an episode of depression or bipolar disorder, you may have a return of symptoms, often called a recurrence or a relapse. A *relapse* is the return of full symptoms after an episode from which you have partially recovered (partial recovery means feeling improved but with a few remaining symptoms). A *recurrence* is the return of full symptoms following an episode from which you have fully recovered. Your chance of having a relapse or recurrence of depression depends in part on how many prior episodes you have had. This means that the more episodes of depression you have experienced, the greater your chance of symptoms returning at some point.

Cognitive behavioral therapy (CBT) has been shown to decrease the chance of relapse. Mindfulness-based cognitive behavioral therapy has also been shown to reduce the risk of relapse and recurrence in some patients. In addition to CBT and other psychotherapy, you can take some preventive steps to manage your own symptoms and in this way improve the quality of your life.

Relapse Prevention is an effective daily approach to help you minimize the chance of a relapse occurring and to help you stay well. Relapse Prevention means that you identify and respond promptly to changes in your Warning Signs, Triggers, or Symptoms of mood disorder. With this strategy, you can intervene when an important change in your emotional health may be happening. Early identification and intervention helps to prevent your episode from worsening.

A Relapse Prevention Strategy includes five main steps that you and your treatment team will act on:

1. Identify your specific Warning Signs, Symptoms, and Triggers (see pages 74–76).
2. Pay attention to changes that are Warning Signs for you.
3. Prepare an intervention Action Plan for Relapse Prevention in advance for use when you notice a change in your Symptoms or Warning Signs. The Action Plan includes steps you will take to manage, cope, and distract from the intensity of the episode. It also includes the people you will ask to help you (health care providers, family, and friends). See page 78.
4. Follow your Action Plan when you first notice a change in your emotional health. An Action Plan enables you to intervene early when necessary and modify or improve the course of the episode.
5. Relapse Prevention also means that you follow some basic *preventive steps* every day. These will help you maintain emotional stability and to decrease your vulnerability to fluctuations, although they may not eliminate these changes completely.

Preventive steps include:

- Maintain good Sleep Hygiene (see pages 8–9).
- Eat three meals per day with balanced nutrition.
- Exercise regularly.
- Keep up with self-care.
- Maintain regular social supports and contacts.
- Avoid isolation.

- Include positive, pleasurable experiences in your life (pages 102–3).
- Keep a structure and routine to your day. Schedule your time (page 24).
- Use your coping skills, the actions you take to lessen the effect of stressors (pages 105–10).
- Remain on your medications as prescribed.
- Do not use alcohol or drugs.
- Continue to work with your psychotherapist.
- Continue to work on any exercises your therapist gives you.

Relapse Prevention for bipolar disorder is very similar. In addition to the recommendations outlined above, a few additional tips are especially helpful to follow:

- Keep your life routine, balanced, and structured.
- Simplify your life as much as possible.
- Avoid overstimulation.
- Pace yourself, breaking large tasks down into several smaller ones.
- Find sources of replenishment and take periodic breaks in the day.
- Decrease chaotic or stimulating input at the end of the day (try relaxing, meditation, writing in your journal, taking a bath).
- Avoid impulsive actions. Wait at least two days before making any major decision or purchase, and ask two trusted friends for their feedback.
- Try social rhythm therapy, which has been formally evaluated as an intervention for bipolar disorder. It can help you keep routine and structure in your day.

Triggers

Triggers are events or circumstances that may cause you distress and lead to an increase in your depression symptoms. It is important to understand that certain circumstances have the potential to set off an episode of depression for you. Triggers can be different for each person, so to be aware of them in your everyday life, you have to first identify them for yourself.

Triggers may include such things as . . .

- external events, good or bad
- a sudden change in your life, such as a loss (of a loved one, job, home, etc.)
- change in a relationship, or a new relationship
- change in daily routine that interrupts familiar patterns (change in sleep, meals, or activities)
- physical illness
- change in medications
- anniversary dates
- traumatic news or event
- good news
- feelings of stress
- feeling overwhelmed
- rejection or criticism (real or perceived)
- embarrassment or guilt
- too many or unwanted responsibilities, obligations, or tasks to do
- change of seasons

Once you have identified what events are Triggers for you, you can figure out with your therapist what steps you can take to minimize their effect on you and improve the situation. You may not be able to change the Trigger, but you can change your response to it. Write your Triggers and these steps in your Action Plan.

Some Triggers for me are . . .

____

____

____

____

____

____

____

____

____

____

____

____

Warning Signs

Warning Signs are distinct changes from your baseline that precede an episode of depression or mania. Each person has a characteristic pattern of Warning Signs. Early recognition of yours gives you a chance to intervene and modify (change or improve) the course of the episode.

Warning Signs may be a noticeable (to you or others) change in your . . .

- thoughts
- feelings
- behaviors
- routine
- self-care

Some examples include a change from your baseline to

- having more negative thoughts
- having problems making decisions, concentrating, solving problems
- feeling more hopeless, worthless, sad, irritable, agitated, anxious, fatigued
- experiencing a lack of energy or interest, a loss of appetite, too much or too little sleep
- having difficulty getting up, going to work, shopping, maintaining your household, handling family responsibilities
- having difficulty preparing meals, eating (too much or too little), maintaining good personal hygiene, doing laundry, handling personal responsibilities

Once you have identified your Warning Signs, work with your therapist to determine the steps you can take to minimize or prevent the episode of depression or mania. Write these steps out in detail in your Action Plan.

Some Warning Signs for me are . . .

____

____

____

____

____

____

____

____

____

An Action Plan for Relapse Prevention

The intervention Action Plan for Relapse Prevention outlines the steps you will take to manage, cope with, and distract from the intensity of an episode of depression or mania. It also lists the people you will ask to help you: health care providers, family, and friends. Research has shown that having a written self-care plan for situations that would lead to a worsening or a recurrence of depression can help manage depression and decrease symptoms. Work with your therapist to develop an intervention Action Plan to use when you or others notice your Warning Signs or a change in your emotional state.

The Action Plan includes the following elements:

- A description of your baseline
- A list of your Triggers
- A list of your Warning Signs
- What to do in response to those Warning Signs
- Names and contact information for your healthcare providers and supportive family and friends
- Useful Coping Strategies
- Suggestions for how others can help

Create your Action Plan now, before you have any intense symptoms, so that you have it ready to use when you or someone else notices your Warning Signs.

Following is a sample Action Plan already filled out to give you an idea of its range of possibilities and how it can be used. Following that you will find a blank form to use for your own care.

Sample Completed ACTION PLAN FOR RELAPSE PREVENTION

My BASELINE

- *Describe your baseline and what you need to do to maintain it.*

When I'm feeling well, I . . .

get up and get showered and dressed every day
go to work and interact with my colleagues
go grocery shopping and prepare my meals
exercise after work and on the weekends—aerobics, jogging, swimming, bicycling, hiking
watch funny movies, read mystery novels, knit
visit with my friends

To stay well, every day I need to . . .

take my medications
sleep 7 hours
eat 3 meals a day
get exercise 5 days a week
see my friends and family or talk to them on the phone
keep up a routine and structure every day

Sample Completed ACTION PLAN FOR RELAPSE PREVENTION

My TRIGGERS

- *List events and situations that can increase your symptoms.*

My father calling up and criticizing me

My boss demanding that I work late

Not getting enough sleep

My WARNING SIGNS

- *List your personal signs, the noticeable changes in thoughts, feelings, behaviors, routine, or self-care that warn of an episode.*

Too little sleep

Skipping meals

Avoiding friends and family

Not getting dressed or showered

Not returning phone calls

Not exercising or going out

Talking too fast

Signature (patient) ____________________ Date __________

Signature (provider) ____________________ Date __________

Sample Completed ACTION PLAN FOR RELAPSE PREVENTION—PART 2

What I will do first when I notice my Warning Signs

☑ Contact my doctor(s) early:

Psychiatrist Dr. Andy Smith tel#

Psychologist/therapist Dr. Tim Jones tel#

Other: Dr. Jon Kelly tel#

☑ Treat any physical medical problems.

☑ Attend to self-care and routine, even if I don't feel like it.

☑ Get enough sleep and eat balanced meals (nutrition).

☑ Take medications as prescribed. Note any recent medication changes.

☑ NO alcohol or drugs.

☐ Other

Supportive persons I will contact (friends, family)

1. Sandi tel#
2. Ginger tel#
3. Joe tel#
4. tel#
5. tel#

Sample Completed ACTION PLAN FOR RELAPSE PREVENTION—PART 2

What I will do to cope, soothe, or distract myself

1. Play piano.
2. Listen to relaxing music.
3. Go to gym.
4. Take bubble bath.
5. Watch funny movies.

What I will *not* do

1. Sit on couch all day.
2. Overeat junk food.
3. Not take a shower.

How other people can help me

1. Listen to me seriously.
2. Call to check on me.
3. Plan something to do.

Signature (patient) ______________________ Date __________

Signature (provider) ______________________ Date __________

ACTION PLAN FOR RELAPSE PREVENTION

My BASELINE

- *Describe your baseline and what you need to do to maintain it.*

When I'm feeling well, I . . .

To stay well, every day I need to . . .

ACTION PLAN FOR RELAPSE PREVENTION

My TRIGGERS

- *List events and situations that can increase your symptoms.*

My WARNING SIGNS

- *List your personal signs, the noticeable changes in thoughts, feelings, behaviors, routine, or self-care that warn of an episode.*

Signature (patient) ______________________ Date __________

Signature (provider) ______________________ Date __________

ACTION PLAN FOR RELAPSE PREVENTION—PART 2

What I will do first when I notice my Warning Signs

❑ Contact my doctor(s) early:

Psychiatrist ______________________ tel# ______________

Psychologist/therapist ______________________ tel# ______________

Other: ______________________ tel# ______________

❑ Treat any physical medical problems.

❑ Attend to self-care and routine, even if I don't feel like it.

❑ Get enough sleep and eat balanced meals (nutrition).

❑ Take medications as prescribed. Note any recent medication changes.

❑ NO alcohol or drugs.

❑ Other

____

____

____

____

Supportive persons I will contact (friends, family)

1. ______________________ tel# ______________
2. ______________________ tel# ______________
3. ______________________ tel# ______________
4. ______________________ tel# ______________
5. ______________________ tel# ______________

ACTION PLAN FOR RELAPSE PREVENTION—PART 2

What I will do to cope, soothe, or distract myself

1.

2.

3.

4.

5.

What I will *not* do

1.

2.

3.

How other people can help me

1.

2.

3.

Signature (patient) ______________________ Date ____________

Signature (provider) ______________________ Date ____________

CHAPTER 6

Cognitive Behavioral Therapy

Thoughts, Feelings, and Behaviors

There is a close connection between our thoughts, feelings, and behaviors (actions). Each of these influences the others. For example, a certain thought may cause you to feel sad. This may then affect your behavior, causing you to cry and withdraw. You then feel more sad. Another thought may cause you to feel anxious, and consequently your behavior is jittery.

Cognitive behavioral therapy (CBT) is a kind of talk therapy (psychotherapy) that addresses this connection between your thoughts, feelings, and behaviors. In CBT you learn to identify and change thinking patterns that may be distorted, beliefs that are inaccurate, and behaviors that are unhelpful. CBT is a way to help you look at your thoughts and determine when you are thinking in a rational or an irrational way. You learn to monitor, challenge, and replace your negative thoughts with more realistic ones and to recognize the connection between your thoughts, feelings, and behaviors. CBT is particularly useful in depression, when your thoughts are often distorted, negative, and upsetting. If you can learn to be more aware of negative thoughts and feelings and respond to them using CBT, then you may be able to avoid a relapse or recurrence of your depression.

*How You **Think** about and Interpret the World Affects How You **Feel***

- People experience the world as a series of events. These events can be positive, negative, or neutral.

- In your mind, you process and *interpret* these events and form thoughts about them. Interpretations are often based on individual beliefs and past experiences.
- Your thoughts give meaning to the event and create feelings about it.
- "Feelings" are created by your thoughts and interpretations of an event and not by the actual event. Thoughts and feelings are not facts.

An event can cause distress depending on how you interpret it in your mind. When you have an *accurate* understanding and interpretation of what is going on around you, your emotions will likely be in a normal range and not usually cause problems. If your thoughts about or interpretations of an event are inaccurate or distorted in some way, the emotions you experience may cause distress. This happens in depression. Challenging these distorted thoughts and interpretations with CBT can improve the way you feel.

What Are Distortions in Your Thoughts?

Distortions in your thoughts are errors in thinking that twist your interpretation of an event in different ways (see the examples in the next section). Many things can make you less accurate in your thinking and interpretation of events, contributing to thought distortions. For example, your thinking can be affected by

- lack of sleep
- poor or imbalanced diet
- substance abuse
- past experiences
- ideas about yourself and the world (your sense of self-worth)
- your mood (such as depression or anxiety)

This may be hard to do when you are depressed. You may feel as though you are describing another person. If you have difficulty with this, get feedback from others who know you well. Ask your friends and family to remind you, honestly, of your strengths and unique personal qualities. Once you identify these qualities, you will have a clearer idea of what you are about, which will help reconnect you to your healthy baseline self. Identifying your preferences and beliefs will help you *be* yourself. Use the worksheets in this chapter to guide you through this exercise.

Perhaps this example will help you get started. When I had trouble writing my own personal statement, my therapist used it as an illustration. In a scene from the movie *Bull Durham*, the baseball character played by the actor Kevin Costner gives us a modified version of this exercise when he confidently states: "I believe in the soul, . . . the hanging curve ball, high fiber, good scotch . . . I believe there ought to be a constitutional amendment outlawing Astroturf and the designated hitter . . . I believe in . . . opening your presents Christmas morning rather than Christmas Eve." He continues on to further list his preferences and opinions. Now we have a deeper idea of who the character is, what he values. Using that as an example, and with input from my friends, I made a list of my own preferences, personal qualities, and values, which we then discussed in session. That list eventually grew and became my responses to the Personal Preferences exercise on page 51.

Step 2

Once you have made your list, *do the things you like,* or used to like, to do. Consciously choose more of your preferences that are "positive" and less of those that are "negative." Work to further develop your strengths and skills.

Step 3

Based on your strengths, beliefs, and preferences, *put together a brief statement about yourself.* This is what you would say to yourself about yourself, your personal narrative. It is not for anyone else to hear right now. Describe who you are, your strengths, and your preferences. "I am a person who ______" is a good place to start.

Sit with it, get used to it, and practice saying it to yourself. Have that statement in your head so that you will have access to it when you need it. Then, when depression comes roaring in, you will have this reminder of who you are, a reminder that you are not defined by your depression. Eventually it will feel comfortable.

Having self-confidence and opinions, having a sense of who you are and having easy access to it, also helps with your relationships.

Sample of a Brief Personal Statement:

> I am a (man, woman) who is intelligent, considerate, and kind, with a subtle sense of humor, respected in my job, caring toward my parents, good at fixing bicycles, who values honesty, integrity, and friendship, and likes baseball, pasta, *Trivial Pursuit,* reading to my daughter, and mystery novels.

Now create your own.

My Personal Statement

I am a person who ______________________________

____

____

____

____

____

____

____

____

PERSONAL PREFERENCES

WHAT I LIKE TO DO WITH MY TIME
Personal and family
Professional
Social and recreational
What would (or used to) give me pleasure?
What would (or used to) give me contentment?
What would (or used to) give me a sense of mastery and competence?

WHAT I WANT IN LIFE
Personal
Professional
Social

WHAT I DO NOT WANT IN LIFE

continued

PERSONAL PREFERENCES *(continued)*

	My Preferred	My Least Preferred
SOCIAL		
People (friends, relatives, etc.)		
Personal characteristics in a friend		
How I like to be treated		
Name I prefer to be called		
People I admire		
People who inspire me		
Topics and causes I care about		
PROFESSIONAL		
What I want from work		
What interests me? What do I like to do?		
I gain satisfaction from . . .		
What kind of environment, workplace, do I like?		
My ideal job would be . . .		

PERSONAL PREFERENCES

	My Preferred	My Least Preferred
PERSONAL		
Activities (What gives me energy? What is fun, interesting, relaxing?)		
Relaxation		
Smells, fragrances		
Colors		
Flowers		
Food		
Beverages		
Restaurants		
Plants, trees		
Seasons		
Views, scenery		
Pets, animals		
Exercise		

continued

PERSONAL PREFERENCES *(continued)*

	My Preferred	My Least Preferred
Sports (participate)		
Sports (watch)		
Vacation		
ART		
Art, artists		
Museums		
Architecture		
Books, authors		
Magazines, newspapers		
Columnist, reporter		
Music—type, performers, composers		
Movies		
Actors		
Television		

Minimizing: discounting the positive aspects of yourself or your actions, insisting they "don't count."

Personalizing: thinking that everything people say or do is a reaction to you personally or assuming total responsibility and blaming yourself for events out of your control.

Blaming: holding other people responsible for your pain or the opposite, blaming yourself as the source of every problem.

Emotional Reasoning: believing that what you feel *must* automatically be true, that negative emotions reflect the true picture. For example, if you *feel* stupid, then you must *be* stupid.

Being Right: being continually on trial and defensive, having to prove that your feelings, opinions, and actions are right. Being wrong is unthinkable. When you think in this way, you will do anything to prove yourself right.

Reward Fallacy: expecting that all your sacrifice and self-denial will pay off, then feeling bitter and resentful when that does not happen.

Source: Adapted in part from David Burns, *Feeling Good: The New Mood Therapy* (New York: Avon, 1980), table 3-1, pp. 42–43.

will show you how to identify the different types of distortions in your thinking and how you can learn to challenge them.

Cognitive behavioral therapy uses a series of exercises to challenge and replace the negative and distorted thoughts that accompany depression. The CBT Mood and Thought Monitoring exercise on page 96 is an effective tool for identifying the automatic distortions in your thoughts that support feelings of distress. When you practice doing this exercise, you can learn to more easily replace the distorted thought with a more accurate, realistic view. This will in turn decrease your level of distress. If this exercise is too difficult for you to do right now, at least remind yourself that you are depressed and that your thoughts may not be accurate at this time.

*How You **Think** and **Feel** also Affects How You **Act***

Your interpretations of the events in your life cause emotions, and in response to these emotions, you also have an urge to act in a certain way. For example, when feeling miserable, you may choose to act angrily, stay in bed, cry, or drink too much alcohol. While some expression of emotion is okay, these are extreme negative behaviors that are not healthy for you.

Since you have the ability to act on your feelings, you also have *some* control over your emotions by choosing *how* to react and respond to them. The actions and decisions you make in response can intensify or lessen a particular feeling. Learning to modify your responses to intense emotion will decrease your level of distress. For example, instead of feeling extremely "enraged" or out of control in response to a troubling situation, you might feel sad or moderately angry. Work with your therapist to learn and practice this skill.

Should Statements

Should statements are things you say that start off with the words "I should . . ." They reflect a rigid set of rules about how you and others must act, think, or feel. These statements take a *desire* and change it to a mandatory, inflexible standard, a moral imperative. When applied to the past, you can never meet that standard of perfection, so you end up feeling guilty, frustrated, or angry.

For example, "I should have been ________________" reflects a situation that can never be met.

Be aware of the "musts," "oughts," "shoulds," and any "standards" you have that others do not share.

Ways to handle should statements:

1. Recognize the standards you cannot reach.
2. Recognize these statements as *desires*, not mandatory rules.

3. Replace thinking "I should ____________" with
   "*I wish I ____________*," or
   "*I would like ____________*"
4. Practice doing this exercise when you catch yourself using a should statement.

Challenging and Changing Your Thoughts

Mood and Thought Monitoring Exercise

The Mood and Thought Monitoring Exercise is an effective CBT tool used to monitor and modify the negative thoughts and emotions that come with depression. In this exercise you will

- look at a particular situation that caused you to feel distress,
- identify the distortions in the thoughts that support those feelings of distress,
- challenge the negative, distorted thoughts, and
- replace them with a more accurate view.

This process, called *cognitive restructuring*, has been found to improve current levels of distress in people struggling with depression. The Mood and Thought Monitoring Exercise is an effective tool to use with your therapist or treatment team. The technique was originally presented by Dr. Aaron T. Beck as the "Daily Record of Dysfunctional Thoughts." It has also been described in detail by Dr. David Burns, in his book *Feeling Good*. The exercise has been widely used clinically and adapted by many others since then.

Purpose of the Mood and Thought Monitoring Exercise

1. Self-assessment
   - To increase your awareness of your thoughts, emotions, feelings, reactions, interpretations

- To understand how your thoughts, feelings, and actions (behaviors) are related and how they affect each other
- To understand what events led up to your current feelings

2. To change your problematic thinking
   - Identify the thoughts that come automatically and support bad feelings (*automatic negative thoughts*) and replace them with a more accurate view of the situation.
   - Identify ways to think differently about yourself and a situation, increase your awareness and perspective, and gain objectivity. Correct errors in your thinking.

How to Use the Mood and Thought Monitoring Exercise

Pick a recent personal experience to think about. Fill in the five columns on the Mood and Thought Monitoring Exercise form on page 96. Then reflect on your thoughts and emotions about the experience. This is not an easy task to do, and it may stir up the emotions you are now thinking about. Review the completed monitoring form with your therapist. Doing this exercise regularly will change your emotions in general, and in particular, those related to each experience. It will eventually improve your mood.

Fill in the Mood and Thought Monitoring Exercise form with your responses to these five steps.

1. Choose a recent situation or event that triggered distressed feelings in you and that is associated with one or more automatic negative thoughts.
2. Notice the emotions associated with that situation (such as sadness, anxiety, fear).
3. Identify the automatic negative thought(s) raised by that situation.
4. Identify the distortions in your thoughts (see Types of Distorted Thinking, on page 90). Replace the distorted, inaccurate thought with a realistic *alternative thought* (this

is called a Rational Response). The alternative thought you choose must be a fair and more accurate view of the situation. It has to be realistic, honest, and believable, and it should validate the emotion you are experiencing.

5. Notice the change in your emotions or in their intensity after you have replaced your thoughts with a more accurate, realistic view.

Example Responses to the Mood and Thought Monitoring Exercise

A situation that triggered thoughts: John did not return my telephone call when he said he would.

Emotions associated with this situation: sadness, anger, rejection . . . at 100 percent intensity.

Automatic negative thoughts: He hates me. He is angry with me. Everybody hates me. I'm a loser. I did something wrong. I'm not important enough.

Distortions in those thoughts: polarized thinking, overgeneralization, mind reading, catastrophizing.

Alternative thought: John is my long-time friend, and he has never given me reason to think he hates me. There is no reason to think he is angry with me that I know of. Some people like me. I do some things right. There is no reason to think that I did something wrong to John. Maybe he is busy or out of town. Maybe he is sick or it slipped his mind.

Emotions after restructuring your thoughts:
sadness: 10 percent intensity; angry: 20 percent intensity; rejected: 10 percent intensity

Notice how the restructured alternative thought has improved the intensity of the initial emotions from 100 percent to 10–20 percent.

MOOD AND THOUGHT MONITORING EXERCISE

Use this form to monitor your mood when you are feeling unpleasant emotion or distress. The purpose is to identify the thoughts you have that support or contribute to the distressed feelings and to help you develop a more accurate view of the situation. Review the completed form with your therapist or treatment team.

Situation	Emotion	Automatic thought
Describe an event, thought, or memory that triggers unpleasant emotion(s) or distress.	Record your current emotion(s) and rate the intensity from 0 to 100 (e.g., anxious, angry, sad, guilty, ashamed).	Record the associated thought(s) you are having that intensify your emotion(s).

Source: Adapted with permission from Aaron T. Beck, A. John Rush, Brian F. Shaw, and Gary Emery, *Cognitive Therapy of Depression* (New York: Guilford Press, 1979), p. 403.

Alternative (rational) response	Emotions after rational response
Identify the distortions in your thought(s). Rewrite the distorted thought as a statement with a fair and more accurate view of the situation.	Record your emotion(s) again and rerate the intensity, 0 to 100.

More Ways to Challenge and Change Your Thinking

- Identify the distortions in your thinking. Use the Types of Distorted Thinking descriptions on page 90 as a guide.
- Use the CBT Mood and Thought Monitoring Exercise to evaluate a situation associated with emotional distress. Substitute a more realistic thought or interpretation of an event for your distorted one.
- Examine the Evidence For and Against a negative thought, belief, or interpretation of an event.
    - Gather evidence.
        - Conduct your own "experiment" and gather evidence to check the accuracy of your thought.
        - Ask others who know you well for their realistic, honest feedback.
        - Seek out experiences that counteract the negative beliefs you have.
    - Ask if your belief is inherently true or if it is an internalized message from your environment.
        - If it is true, what is in your power to change?
- Examine the pros and cons of any thought, belief, decision, or action.
- When a thought or belief is upsetting you, look at whether your thought and reaction have more to do with events from long ago. Ask yourself:
    - Where does this thought come from?
    - Does it apply *now,* in the current situation?
- Separate your opinion and interpretation from fact. Interpretations often distort a situation negatively.
- Avoid making judgments or interpretations. Feelings and interpretations are not facts.
    - Rely on the facts. Ask yourself: Is this an interpretation, or is it a *fact?*

- Replace should statements with less demanding language, such as "I would like it if . . ."
- Instead of assuming full responsibility and blame for a particular problem, consider other factors that might have contributed, that were outside your control.
- Use the same compassion in talking to yourself as you would give to others.
- Try thinking of things in the middle ground, or gray area, instead of at the extremes of black and white.

Evidence For and Against

When a thought, belief, or interpretation of an event is troubling, it is often helpful to examine the Evidence For and Against that thought. The evidence you gather will help you identify and change thoughts that are based on inaccurate assumptions.

Step 1. Identify a belief or thought that is negative or upsetting.

Step 2. Gather Evidence For and Against that thought.

- Collect specific evidence about that thought to check its accuracy
- Ask others who know you well for their realistic, honest feedback about that thought
- Seek out experiences that counteract your negative beliefs. This means that you go out and do something to see first-hand the evidence against your negative belief.

Step 3. Look at your list realistically and see where the evidence lies.

Ask yourself if your belief is inherently true or if it is an internalized message from your environment. If you find it is true, ask yourself what is in your power to change?

EVIDENCE FOR AND AGAINST

Belief or thought	Evidence for it	Evidence against it

UNDERSTANDING THE ORIGINS OF YOUR THOUGHTS

Sometimes the thoughts that bother us come from situations long ago, but the thoughts stay with us, even though they no longer apply. Spending time reacting to old thoughts does not help your current situation.

Ask whether your distressed thought or reaction applies to the current situation or to events in your past. Does it apply now? If it does not apply now, try to put it aside.

Distressed thought or reaction	Where does that come from?	Does it apply now?

Pleasure and Mastery

Add some Pleasure and Mastery activities to your week, even if you don't feel like it or don't feel that you deserve it. It is not enough to eliminate negative experiences from your life. You also need to have positive and pleasurable experiences. Pleasurable activities will help decrease the chance of your depression symptoms getting worse. They are a way to help yourself, part of your Relapse Prevention plan.

Create a list of pleasurable activities that you like to do, or used to like to do. Choose to do some of these regularly, and add them to your schedule.

Next, list activities you like that challenge you, that provide you with a feeling of competence and effectiveness. They should be a little difficult for you to do (such as overcoming an obstacle or learning a new skill). These are called Mastery activities. Choose to do some of these on a regular basis, and add them to your schedule.

Pleasurable Experiences

We each have our own preferences for pleasurable activities. Here are some examples:

- Relax (on your own or using a relaxation tape)
- Stretch
- Get physical exercise
- Go for a walk outdoors
- Enjoy the weather
- Bicycle
- Garden
- Play a sport
- Watch sports
- Play a game
- Spend time with friends
- Spend time with family you enjoy
- Spend time with children
- Volunteer
- Do a jigsaw puzzle
- Do Sudoku
- Do a crossword puzzle
- Play with a pet

Listen to music

Attend a concert

Play an instrument

Sing

Learn a new language

Look at beautiful scenery

Look at beautiful art

Go to a museum

Enjoy a good fragrance or other smell

Indulge in self-care (bubble bath, etc.)

Get a massage

Get your hair done

Have a manicure or pedicure

Cook

Eat a good meal

Go on a date

Enjoy quiet time

Meditate

Work on a favorite project

Learn something new

Reach a goal

Travel

Work on a favorite hobby

Read a good book or magazine

Read the comics

Plan a party

Go to a party

Give someone a gift

Watch a good or funny movie

Laugh

Shop or window shop

Knit, crochet, do needlepoint

Do woodworking, other crafts

Build something

And lots of other things . . .

What is pleasurable for me?

____

____

____

____

____

PLEASURE AND MASTERY

Pleasure Activities

- *Things I like (or used to like) to do . . .*

Mastery Activities

- *Things I like (or used to like) to do that challenge me and give a sense of competence and accomplishment . . .*

CHAPTER 7

Strategies to Get You through the Tough Times

The life skills described in this chapter can help you through some of the rough times. A few of the approaches are a review from previous chapters, included here as a reminder because they can be difficult to remember and do when depressed. You will learn strategies for Coping and Stress, Mindfulness, and Distress Tolerance. In addition, there is an overview of Communication Skills, with recommendations for Dealing with Family and Friends and Talking with Your Doctor, as well as Tips for Family and Friends.

Coping and Stress

Stress is an emotionally and physically disturbing condition you may have in response to challenging life events. When you are suffering from depression, dealing with stress can be more difficult. It can also make your depression worse and contribute to relapse, or a return of symptoms.

Stress can come from events inside or outside you. The causes and intensity of stress may vary from person to person, but common causes include:

- real events in life (positive or negative, e.g., marriage, divorce, birth, job, finances, a major loss)
- relationships
- an illness
- change (of any kind)
- your environment

- overload of responsibilities
- an unresolved conflict
- a situation not under your control
- uncertainty while waiting on an unknown outcome

You can actively take steps to lessen the effects of stress and decrease your vulnerability to stressors. This is called *coping*. When you manage stress using effective Coping Strategies, you decrease the negative effect that stress has on your depression.

Coping Strategies include ways to prevent and prepare for stress as well as skills for managing it when it occurs:

1. Maintain a regular schedule and structure of activities. This includes optimizing your sleep, diet and nutrition, exercise, and self-care.

2. Manage the little daily stressors.
    - Prioritize your responsibilities and activities.
    - Keep yourself organized.
    - Maintain a schedule but don't overschedule, and adjust as needed.
    - Break down large or complex tasks into smaller pieces that are more manageable.
    - Keep a to-do list and a daily reminders list.
    - Write things down in a notebook, including healthcare-related questions and instructions.
    - Use a daily pillbox for your medications, to keep track of when you took them.
    - Develop a system that you like and that works for you to manage the mail, bills, and housekeeping.
    - Avoid overstimulation.
    - Be mindful, in this moment.

3. Use CBT strategies. An event can cause stress depending on how you interpret it in your mind. Usually we interpret events based on individual beliefs and past experiences.

Sometimes we also interpret events with distortions in our thinking. Challenging these distorted thoughts and interpretations using cognitive behavioral therapy can affect the way you feel and respond and can improve your level of stress.

- Use the CBT exercises (see chapter 6).
- Keep a journal of your thoughts and feelings.
- Identify the sources of your stress. This will help you respond to it in a more effective way, when you know what you are dealing with.
- Be assertive in your communication—this helps you to feel in control of your situation.
- Keep your perspective.

4. Use problem-solving strategies.
    - Speak with someone (a friend, therapist) for help as you work out a problem.
    - Get accurate information about the problem to make an informed decision.
    - Evaluate and define the situation realistically.
    - Consider your options and the alternatives.
    - List the pros and cons of your options.
    - Seek additional assistance as needed.
5. Distract and refocus your attention.
    - Occupy your mind with other thoughts and activities: puzzles, reading, hobbies, sports, gardening, or other things you like to do.
    - Volunteer your time; reach out to others.
    - Replace your current emotion with another (e.g., by watching a movie or reading a book that is funny or scary).
    - Leave the situation aside mentally for a while.

Coping Strategies

Try any of these examples of Coping Strategies to find what works for you. The more familiar you are with your options, the easier it will be to remember them during stressful times or an episode of depression or mania.

- Ask for help.
- Don't give up.
- Do the best with what you have available to you now.
- Focus on what matters.
- Seek a solution to the problem.
- Seek out the facts. Identify and challenge any inaccurate assumptions and interpretations.
- List your options.
- Examine the Evidence For and Against.
- Try an alternative approach, a different way of thinking.
- Anticipate, think, and plan ahead.
- Be active, not passive.
- Be assertive.
- Listen to your needs.
- Say "no" when necessary.
- Get organized.
- Control what you can.
- Set realistic and specific goals.
- Balance and prioritize.
- Pace yourself.
- Don't overcommit.
- Structure your day.
- Take good care of your body (sleep, diet, exercise).

- Treat yourself with compassion and respect.
- Focus on the present moment.
- Use self-soothing.
- Give yourself credit.
- Reward yourself.
- Stay safe. Avoid situations that could worsen your symptoms.
- Consider the consequences of your actions and decisions.
- Watch for your Triggers and Warning Signs. Activate your Action Plan for Relapse Prevention as needed.
- Develop some Distress Tolerance (using distraction, self-soothing, improving the moment; see page 113).

---

6. Try relaxation techniques (work with your therapist to learn these skills).
    - Progressive muscle relaxation—relax each muscle in your body from head to toe, one muscle group at a time (start with your jaw, then move to your neck, shoulders, arms, fingers, etc.).
    - Visualization—sit and focus on a calm, serene image or a place where you feel relaxed.
    - Biofeedback—discuss with your therapist how to learn this technique.
    - Meditation—Dr. Herbert Benson's book *The Relaxation Response* gives detailed information on getting started.
    - Deep breathing exercise—sit quietly and focus only on your breathing, taking slow deep breaths. Do this for 3 to 5 minutes. If your mind wanders, refocus on each breath.
7. Use humor: watch a funny movie or DVD, read a funny book, read the comics. Being able to appreciate humor is a healthy coping strategy.

8. Use self-soothing strategies: comfort and nurture yourself with gentleness and kindness, using the five senses:
   - *Vision:* enjoy looking at flowers, art, or other objects of beauty; visit museums; get out in nature; see a play, musical, or dance production.
   - *Taste:* have a favorite food or beverage; take it slow and savor the experience.
   - *Smell:* use a favorite fragrance or lotion; buy flowers or walk through a flower garden or shop; bake cinnamon rolls or cookies.
   - *Touch:* take a bubble bath, get a massage, wear comfortable fabrics, hug someone.
   - *Hearing:* listen to beautiful, soothing music or sounds of nature; sing; play an instrument.
9. Use Mindfulness techniques (see below)
   - Focus on the present moment, on purpose, nonjudgmentally.
   - Focus on doing one thing at a time, in just this moment.
   - Avoid ruminating about the past or worrying about the future.

Mindfulness

Mindfulness is a way of living your life by focusing on the present moment. It is a way of "being" in the world, adopted from Eastern meditation practices. The skills learned in Mindfulness practice have been found helpful in managing mood disorders.

As described by Jon Kabat-Zinn, Mindfulness means being in the present moment in a particular way, by

- paying attention
- on purpose
- nonjudgmentally

Being in the present moment means that instead of being preoccupied with the past or future, you are focused on and attentive to the present. This is not easy to do. It is common for the mind to wander, particularly to thoughts of past events or future worries. The key is to notice when your thoughts drift and then bring your mind back to the present. Becoming so deeply involved in doing something that you lose track of time is an example of being in the present moment.

Mindfulness requires that you *pay attention* to what is going on around you. It means that you live with awareness instead of going through life on autopilot. Paying attention also involves observing your own thoughts and feelings, your body's response to emotion (such as rapid heart rate, sweating, etc.), your urges, and your behavior just as they are.

Being *nonjudgmental* means that you avoid making any judgment about your thoughts, actions, or experiences and let each moment be as it is. Allow yourself to think or feel what you are feeling, without putting labels or judgment on it. This is also not easy to do. Part of your mind is constantly evaluating your experiences, comparing them to past experiences or expectations you may have. Instead, work on developing a neutral attitude toward what comes into your mind without judging it. Acknowledge your thoughts as thoughts and then let them go. For each experience, emotion, or thought you have, try to feel it without reacting to it.

Why Practice Mindfulness?

- Living mindfully allows you to engage in what you are doing. Emotions will interfere less often. This will improve the quality of your life.
- Mindfulness helps you to live in the present moment instead of experiencing the painful emotions related to the past or future. Dwelling on past experiences or future worries tends to trigger painful emotions. This happens often in depression. Mindfulness practice helps you to decrease these ruminations and the emotions and distress they produce.

- Mindfulness practice can help you manage your mood disorder. When you have an increased awareness of the present moment, you are able to notice when symptoms of your mood disorder arise. Recognizing your depression or bipolar symptoms enables you to respond effectively with your Relapse Prevention plan.
- Mindfulness can improve your ability to tolerate and respond to painful events. When you are overwhelmed by emotions, your mind clutters up quickly. So you have to focus first on the thought or moment and try to clear your mind, to calm it down. To do this you must step back, observe your own thought, and try to get a handle on it. Mindfulness practice can help you do this. When you are focused on and attentive to the present moment, without attaching judgment or value to it, you can make the best use of your thoughts, take action, and work on your problem.
- Many people find that Mindfulness-based cognitive behavioral therapy is an effective treatment for depression.

How Do You Practice Mindfulness?

Mindfulness is a skill that you can develop with practice. Begin by trying to make yourself more aware of the present moment without judging it as good or bad. Focus your full attention on what you are doing, on one thing at a time. Get fully involved in that moment. Notice when your mind wanders and bring your attention back to the moment. You can begin to practice this by setting aside five minutes a day to do a Mindfulness meditation (see below).

You can also try to exercise Mindfulness as you go about your day. For example, when you brush your teeth, focus your mind on doing only that one task. Pay attention to your actions, to the taste, sensations, sounds, and so on. As your mind wanders, bring it back to the task of brushing your teeth in this moment. Try it again when you drive, wash the dishes, have a conversation, or during other moments of your life. Live with awareness of what you are doing instead of going through life automatically.

Exercise to Practice Being Mindful

1. Sit in a comfortable chair, in a comfortable position.
2. Close your eyes if you like.
3. Become aware of your breathing, and focus on each breath.
4. Anchor your attention to the present moment: pay attention to your breathing, the sounds around you, the physical sensations you have.
5. Observe what you feel, see, and hear without placing a value or judgment on it.
6. Continue to focus on each breath, in and out.
7. When intrusive thoughts come into your mind, let them go without judging them or yourself. Return your focus to your breathing. Over time it will become easier to focus your mind in this way.

Distress Tolerance

Sometimes the intensity of depression is so deep, it feels like a crisis situation. You may feel a sense of urgency or a desire to act impulsively. You may feel there is no way out. These feelings can interfere with your efforts to manage depression and maintain stability. Learning to tolerate distress for a short time can help you get through a difficult moment, when you cannot change the situation. Distress Tolerance strategies help you do this by using skills to distract yourself, soothe yourself, provide solace, and improve the difficult moment.

These strategies are not a cure for the problems of life. They are not meant to dismiss the seriousness of your problems. Practicing Distress Tolerance is more like taking a break from your situation for a short while. Use these skills when you feel overwhelmed by your depression. Eventually the intensity of the moment will fade away.

Strategies to Achieve Distress Tolerance

Distraction

Decrease your contact with events that trigger distress using:

- Activities, such as hobbies, sports, or gardening, to distract your attention
- Other thoughts or sensations to distract your mind (such as by doing puzzles, reading)
- Contribution—reach out, volunteer, find a sense of meaning
- Comparison—with those less fortunate
- Emotions—replace a current emotion with another one (such as by watching a funny or scary movie)

Note: Keep in mind that short-term distraction is not the same as avoiding a problem. Don't push away—avoidance is not helpful as a regular strategy.

Self-Soothing

Be kind to yourself and provide comfort and nurturing by engaging the five senses:

- *Vision:* enjoy looking at flowers, art, or other objects of beauty; visit museums; get out in nature; see a play, musical, or dance production.
- *Taste:* have a favorite food or beverage; take it slow and savor the experience.
- *Smell:* use a favorite fragrance or lotion; buy flowers or walk through a flower garden or shop; bake cinnamon rolls or cookies.
- *Touch:* take a bubble bath, get a massage, wear comfortable fabrics, hug someone.
- *Hearing:* listen to beautiful, soothing music or sounds of nature; sing; play an instrument.

Note: Some people feel they are not deserving, or they feel guilt or shame when using self-soothing strategies. If these are problems for you, work on them with your therapist or treatment team.

Improve the Moment

To replace the immediate negative event with a positive experience or image, try the following:

- Visualization—sit and focus on a calm, serene image or a place where you feel relaxed
- Meditation—Dr. Herbert Benson's book *The Relaxation Response* gives detailed information on getting started
- Focusing on one thing in the moment (see the Mindfulness section of this chapter, on page 110, and the following exercise)
- Breathing exercise—sit quietly and focus only on your breathing, taking slow deep breaths, for 3 to 5 minutes; if your mind wanders, refocus on each breath
- Prayer
- Relaxation techniques
- Encouraging self-talk (be your own cheerleader)
- Thinking of pros and cons—the positive and negative aspects of tolerating distress

Basic Principles of Distress Tolerance

- Tolerating distress requires the ability to accept yourself and the current situation.
- Acceptance does not mean you approve of the distressing situation. It is not the same as judging it good.
- Acceptance is a skill for tolerating and surviving the crisis in the moment, until the intensity fades. It will fade.

Communication Skills

With depression, speaking up and advocating for yourself can be hard to do. You may feel that your needs, feelings, or opinions are not important or deserving. However, symptoms of depression can worsen if you hold things inside when you are upset and don't talk about what you want and need. This can also lower your self-esteem. It is important to communicate clearly and effectively so that the other person really *hears* you. Your style of communication determines whether and how your message is received. Communication styles can be described as aggressive, assertive, passive, or a combination (passive-aggressive).

An aggressive communication style is dominating, with yelling, threats, and anger. It is not effective. Aggressiveness tends to alienate the other person, making him or her defensive. You don't accomplish what you want with this communication style, and you don't feel good about yourself.

A passive style, where you remain quiet and submissive, is also not effective. When you are passive, you don't speak up to make your needs and wants known. When you do not speak up and advocate for yourself, you run the risk of doing and becoming what the other person wants you to do and be. Your needs and wants are not met. The other person responds in a way that is not in your best interest, and you do not accomplish your goals. You then have no control over what happens to you and often feel worse about yourself.

Being assertive means that you stand up for yourself in a calm, confident manner. You express your beliefs, opinions, wants, and needs effectively and do what you believe is right. With this communication style, you have a greater chance of being able to negotiate what you want and need. When you are assertive, you feel better about yourself for stating what you want, need, or feel. Self-esteem improves, and you have an increased sense of control over what happens to you.

Dealing with Family and Friends

For many people, one of the toughest, most stressful parts of a having mood disorder is discussing the illness with their family and friends. Personal relationships surrounding your illness usually fall into three categories:

1. People you choose to tell about your mood disorder who are mainly supportive
2. People who know about it and are not supportive
3. People you choose not to tell (such as a distant acquaintance or an employer)

Most individuals with mood disorders have a variety of these relationships to manage, and you are not alone if you feel that a family member does not understand your illness or what you are going through. In fact, many loved ones have a hard time understanding this illness. William Styron experienced it this way: "Depression is a disorder of mood, so mysteriously painful and elusive . . . as to verge close to being beyond description. It thus remains nearly incomprehensible to those who have not experienced it in its extreme mode." He understands the challenge that is facing you, trying to bring your loved ones on board to something that may be difficult for them to understand.

It is important to protect your own health by managing these relationships well. The question is, how do you get through these stressful encounters? The first step is to remind yourself that you have an illness that is treatable, and that you are doing your best to manage it. Understand the nature of your illness, its ups and downs, and your patterns. Use your treatment team wisely as a support. Then try to increase the level of understanding about the illness among your friends and family. Offer them books to read, have them come to a family meeting with your therapist, or ask them to attend a community lecture or presentation with you on mood disorders.

Assertiveness

These guidelines can help you learn to communicate assertively, and therefore more effectively:

- Speak up. Believe you have the right to what you want and need.
- Be clear, concise, and firm.
- Appear confident in voice, tone, and manner.
- Use a calm, neutral voice. The tone you use can change your message (the most common tones people use are angry, nasty, meek, passive, aggressive, and neutral).
- Use neutral body language, because body position can change your message.
  - Sit up straight, with an open, relaxed posture and easy manner.
  - Make eye contact.
  - Do not cross your arms, point a finger, make a fist, or fidget.
- Express your feelings, opinions, and wishes.
- Use statements, not questions.
- Use "I" statements, such as "I would like . . ." and "I feel . . ."
- Do not make accusations or threats. Do not say "You did," "You should," etc. That empowers the other person and makes him or her defensive.
- Focus on your objectives and avoid straying from the topic.
- It may help to plan what you will say in advance and write it down.
- Listen to the other person. Try to validate and understand his or her position as well.
- Ask questions to clarify what you do not understand.
- Negotiate a solution that maintains your integrity and values.

- You do not have to respond to the other person in the moment of emotion. It is okay to say, "Let me gather my thoughts and discuss this later," and then do it when you feel calmer.
- Don't expect to be always aware of or able to handle your thoughts and feelings immediately, in the midst of discussion or emotion. It's okay to respond later on by saying, "I've thought about this for a while and . . ."

Family and Friends Who Are Supportive

These are the close, important people in your life, and they should be the ones you turn to during the good and not-so good times. They should be your regular social contacts and the people you reach out to as part of your Action Plan for Relapse Prevention (for when things get worse—see chapter 5). Do not hesitate to open up to them about your illness and tell them what you are feeling, even if you are feeling suicidal. Try to have more than one person in this category, because anyone can be away or busy with life's obligations at any given moment.

Family and Friends Who Are Not Supportive

Remember that not everyone is able to understand or come to terms with a mood disorder for their own reasons, which are not related to you personally. Often other people respond to your illness based on something inside themselves, not you. Some people incorrectly believe in a stigma about your illness and can see it only as shameful and socially unacceptable. They may be judgmental and critical of you, believing you to be incompetent, weak in character, or undesirable because you have a mood disorder. But this is all because of their own ill-informed belief system about mental health.

Their reactions probably feel hurtful to you, because you want your loved ones to be on your side, to fully understand your illness and what you are going through. In these situations, you need to step back and understand that you may never be able to change

Listening

Listening is a communication skill that is important to maintaining your relationships. With depression, the thought distortions and lack of concentration can affect your ability to listen well and communicate clearly and effectively. Practice using these recommendations to improve your ability to listen and to relate well in your relationships.

- Make eye contact.
- Use open, neutral body language: sit up straight, with an inviting, relaxed posture.
- Give your full attention.
- Show genuine interest.
- Smile. Be relaxed and warm. Use humor.
- Validate and acknowledge the other person's experience (e.g., nod your head). Do not be dismissive, make assumptions, refer to your own personal experiences, or give advice.
- Periodically summarize what the other person says.
  For example:
  "It appears that _____," "It sounds like _____,"
  "What you seem to be saying is _____."
  "Is that the case? Do I understand correctly?"
- Clarify the other person's points and comments.
- Offer feedback—share what you thought, felt, and sensed in the conversation without being judgmental. Be honest and supportive.

Some things can get in the way of effective listening. Be aware of times when you might make these mistakes. This will help you improve your listening skills.

Blocks to effective listening include:

- Making assumptions (without the facts)

- Filtering out what the person is saying (when you avoid hearing some of the details)
- Changing the subject to yourself or another topic
- Comparing the person's experience to another experience
- Mind reading (when you conclude, without the facts, that you know what the other person is thinking)
- Rehearsing (when you focus on what you are going to say next)
- Judging what the other person is saying
- Identifying (when you refer to your own similar experience)
- Daydreaming, not paying attention
- Giving advice
- Sparring, put-downs, sarcasm, debating a point
- Having to be right at any length
- Placating the other person

---

the other person's opinion no matter how hard you try. You may need to "agree to disagree" on this matter if you want to continue the relationship. Remember that the people who respond in this way do still love you in their own way. They are just not capable of accepting your illness at this point in their lives.

So how do you deal with them?

- Try for a family meeting with your therapist and see if that helps.
- Do not expect to receive the kind of support from them that you might receive from other, more supportive persons.
- You may choose to limit your conversations with them to other topics, not your illness.
- You might choose to limit the amount of contact you have with this nonsupportive individual, in person, on the

telephone, or by e-mail. This is particularly important if your interactions are upsetting to you.

- Unfortunately, sometimes relationships, particularly new friendships, are lost when one has a mood disorder. This is painful, but again, try not to take it personally. The lost friendship is related to the other person's inability to deal with the illness, not you.

People You Choose Not to Tell

You have every right to keep your illness confidential and disclose it only to those closest to you. This is advisable in many situations, such as for people you have just met or recent acquaintances you do not know very well. You may also choose to keep it private from your employer and co-workers. This depends on your work situation, the type of work you do, the length of time you have worked there, your relationship with your boss, your seniority in your job, and many other factors. You may just decide to take an "extended lunch" for a doctor's appointment and say nothing more. It is all up to you—there is no right or wrong answer here.

If your illness is beginning to interfere with your job performance, however, it may then be preferable to disclose it confidentially to your employer so that he or she has a realistic understanding of why your previously outstanding work has slipped. Then together you might decide to modify your duties, change to a part-time schedule, or take some time off while you recover. You may be surprised to find out that most employers would understand.

Talking with Your Doctor

A good working relationship with your treatment team (psychiatrist, clinical psychologist or therapist) is essential to managing your depression or bipolar disorder. Your treatment is a collaboration between you and your health care providers. You must be able to communicate well with each other so that your needs are understood and met. This includes taking the time to ask questions and make your concerns known.

Come prepared for your appointments by writing down in advance . . .

- any new problems, side effects, or issues since the last visit
- questions you would like to ask
- topics or treatments to clarify or review
- a list of current medications and dosages (include nonprescription vitamins and herbal supplements and information about your medication allergies and any significant adverse reactions to medications you have had)

Be sure to prioritize your issues. Understand that not everything can be covered in one session. You might find it helpful to use a small notebook for recording the above information as well as treatment instructions in detail, homework assignments, appointments, information about past medications, and so forth. To communicate effectively during the appointment, follow these guidelines:

- Speak up. Let your doctor know what issues are important to you.
- Try to be as clear, concise, and accurate as possible.
- Ask questions. For example:
  - What is wrong with me? What is my diagnosis?
  - What treatment or medications do you recommend and why?
  - Are there other treatment options?
  - What are the benefits and risks of this treatment?
  - How long will it take to know if this treatment is effective?
  - How should I expect to feel with this medication? What side effects might I have?
- When you receive instructions from your doctor, write them down in detail. It is often difficult to listen and remember complex information.

- Ask your doctor to repeat or clarify points or instructions you do not understand or remember, or that seem vague or uncertain. Do not leave the appointment if you are unclear about any instructions.
- Don't be embarrassed if you forget or do not understand something. No question is "dumb."
- Don't be concerned that your provider will be "angry" with you or will refuse to answer your question.
- People differ in the amount of information or detail they want to know about their illness. Some may only want a basic overview, while others feel more in control of what is happening to them when they know the facts. Decide what is best for you and let your doctor know.

If you have a problem communicating with your doctor, state your concern as honestly and openly as possible, in a nonthreatening manner, without making accusations. For example, you might say . . .

- "I'm concerned that we aren't communicating as well as we could, such as when ______."
- "I need to be able to talk with you about ______, and I feel like I can't. Can we discuss this?"
- "I would like to discuss ______ at more length. Can we schedule a time for that?"
- "I am having trouble understanding ______. Can you help me understand?"

Tips for Family and Friends

What should I say? What can I do to help?

We each have our own way of coping with stressful situations and illness. We have our own set of personal experiences with illness, relationships, life events, and work. Because of these differences, people have varying needs, and there are many ways to offer help.

Do try to:

- Be present and give your full attention; have your mind "in the moment."
- Listen. This sounds simple, but it may be hard to do. You don't always have to respond. Sometimes an empathetic listener is what the person needs the most.
- Let him or her know that you care. Be mindful that greater patience and compassion may be called for during certain times.
- Validate the person's feelings. Make him or her feel they are worthwhile.
- If you want to offer encouragement, remind the person of his or her special qualities (like a sense of humor) and other successfully managed challenges or accomplishments.
- Know the symptoms of depression, mania, and suicide risk.
- Be aware of the person's Warning Signs, which precede a worsening episode of depression or mania, and know when to encourage the call for help.
- Respect a person's choice about how much he or she wants to share. Some people are very private while others will talk more about their depression. If someone confides in you, keep the conversation private. Ask how much the person wants others to know.
- If asked, be available to help the person talk through treatment decisions, but do not offer advice. Respect decisions about treatment even if you disagree.
- Offer to help with routine tasks, but do not take over. Look for ways to encourage and facilitate the person's self-care.
- Offer to help in concrete, specific ways (pick up grocery items, walk the dog, go with him or her to an appointment).
- Include the person in the usual activities and social events. Let him or her be the one to determine if something is too much to manage.

- Keep your relationship as normal and balanced as possible. The person may appreciate conversations and activities that don't involve depression.
- Expect the person to have good days and bad days, emotionally and physically.

Do not:

- Offer advice or be judgmental.
- Compare the person's experience to others you have known.
- Automatically offer reassuring words when someone expresses despair or a dark emotion. Before saying, "you'll be fine," think about whether you are saying this to calm your own anxiety and fear. Sometimes it can cause the person to feel dismissed rather than supported.
- Take things too personally. It's not uncommon for the person to be more quiet or irritable than usual.
- Be afraid to talk about depression or mania or to ask about suicidal thoughts.

CHAPTER 8

Pulling It All Together

What does it look like and feel like to manage your depression successfully, to actually do everything mentioned so far in this book? The strategies are not a magical cure for depression. But they will help you get through the illness with episodes that are perhaps less intense.

The first thing you experience when you manage your depression is being able to go about your day with an acceptance that depression is an illness, one that can be treated and managed. It is not a weakness or a character flaw. When you manage your illness, you do not listen to those who offer misinformed comments or unhelpful advice. This is a big relief for many people. You know that as part of the illness, your mood will change up and down, and that you will have good days and not-so-good days. You try to understand the fluctuations and patterns you experience. Some days you will wake up feeling relatively okay, and other days, you will feel absolutely down. That is the time to remind yourself even more that the down times are part of the picture and that this moment will eventually pass. This is not easy to do.

When you manage your depression well, you follow the Basics of Mental Health each day. This will help you stay well mentally and physically. Managing your depression means you keep up with personal self-care and follow the treatment plan set up by your providers. You sleep 7 to 8 hours every night, eat a balanced diet of healthy food three times a day, limit caffeine and tobacco intake, and do not use alcohol or street drugs. It means that you take all your medications as prescribed, even if you are feeling better. It includes getting some form of exercise each day, depending on your physical limits.

Another essential piece of managing your depression well is to avoid isolation. You do this by keeping up with your family and friends and other social contacts, even when you don't really feel like it. If you have not heard from someone in a while, you pick up the phone and call the person. Sometimes other people do not know what to say to you when you feel very depressed, so they may not call for fear of feeling awkward or uncomfortable. At those times, it is important for you to initiate the contact, to keep up those friendships that will sustain you.

Following the Basics of Mental Health means that you structure your day and follow a routine. You get up and dressed at the same time each day and have several things planned, written down in a calendar or agenda book. You pace yourself with a realistic number of activities that you can accomplish. These include your responsibilities and obligations, pleasurable and positive experiences, and mastery experiences (see chapter 4). You understand that it is not helpful for you to stay in bed or on the couch all day, with endless hours of free time on your hands. You know how difficult it is to go to work or be active when you are depressed and tired and don't have an interest in anything. The best advice is to do it anyway, and motivation will eventually follow. Many people have found that they start off feeling too tired to do something, but when they become engaged in the project, the fatigue seems to get better or disappear.

Managing your depression effectively requires that you pay attention to your symptoms and monitor them. You are aware of your specific Warning Signs and Triggers for worsening depression. You have made a plan with your treatment team to intervene when a change in these signs becomes problematic. Managing your illness well also means that you take steps to minimize the chance of relapse occurring. You do this by following the basic preventive steps mentioned above, which will help you maintain emotional stability and decrease your vulnerability to fluctuations. You learn to use effective coping skills in the short and long term to help get you through the rough patches. This means that you identify in advance what is pleasurable, relaxing, and distracting for you and are ready to engage in those activities when needed. You use problem-solving techniques and avoid negative behaviors.

All of the above prepares you to do the really hard work of managing depression, which is learning how to control the negative, distorted thoughts and self-talk that seem to dominate your mind and upset you. This is not easy to do, and it may take years to develop the skill. You learn to identify a negative thought when it appears and understand that it is the depression talking, that it is not a fact. You learn to challenge the negative thought and replace it with a more realistic one. When you understand the source of the negative thought, you take away the power it has over your thinking and in turn your mood.

You may wonder how you can follow these recommendations to manage your illness when you are depressed and feel no hope. It is helpful for you to believe in the exercises to get the most benefit from them, but not essential. Do them anyway. If you do not feel hopeful about your future, *borrow some hope* from a person you respect, who knows and understands you. Tell yourself, "Jon believes there is hope for me and he is no fool." Eventually you will find that the hope is your own.

None of this comes easily, but with continued effort and practice you will be able to manage your depression and increase your chance of staying well.

CHAPTER 9

Collective Wisdom

Advice from Some Remarkable People

"Do not buy into these [negative, distorted] thoughts. Not fair to believe them. Wait it out."—TJP

"The time you are feeling the worst is not the time to give up." —AAN

"Feelings are not fact. Interpretation is not fact. Judgment is not fact. STOP. Look at the facts. Then modify your assessment/ interpretation of the situation."—TJP

"With depression, feeling 'good' is alien and may feel uncomfortable at first. You are not used to it and may feel anxious. The brain sees it as different and 'not right,' so the tendency is to go back. Don't. You have to push yourself."—MJ

"Practice consciously endorsing yourself."—MJ

"Action precedes motivation."—mantra of the McLean Hospital MAP Program (original source: Robert J. McKain)

"Sometimes we experience a combination of physical, emotional, and interpersonal symptoms for such a long time that we don't even recognize them as symptoms. We get used to them and think they are normal."—Marjorie Hansen Shaevitz

"Courage doesn't always roar. Sometimes courage is the quiet voice at the end of the day saying 'I will try again tomorrow.'" —Mary Anne Radmacher

"You cannot absorb praise unless you decide to believe and validate what is being said."—MGH psychiatry resident

"There is Hope because . . . we see you in a different way than you see yourself, and if you were to see yourself as we see you, then you could believe and hope that life could be different."
—JEA

"That is just the way you have come to regard yourself. It is not necessarily true."—APS

Do not buy into these [negative, distorted] thoughts. Not fair to believe them. Wait it out.

A very wise clinical psychologist reminded me of this one day when I was feeling particularly low and hopeless about my situation, overwhelmed with negative thoughts, which he believed were untrue and distorted. My depressed brain believed these thoughts were true and would last forever, something that is common in depression. It was easier to believe these thoughts than to do the work of challenging them, particularly when so depressed.

His point was that these thoughts were the depression talking, and that they would not last forever. He said that it was not fair to me to believe something that was not true, something that was based on the disease, even though my brain was trying to tell me otherwise. He asked me to be patient and wait until the negative, distorted thoughts passed. This was not easy to do, but with our work together and time, they eventually did. I try to remind myself of this each time the negative thoughts become intrusive.

The time you are feeling the worst is not the time to give up!

Again, this advice came from an extraordinarily wise and clever psychiatrist at a dark and hopeless time in my life. I was ready to call it quits, and he was just *not* going to let that happen. He wrote this statement on a paper prescription pad and signed it. I still keep the paper in my wallet. His point was that we should not make major life decisions, such as giving up, when we are very down and depressed, at our lowest point. When you are feeling the worst, you are not in a position to make the best decisions for yourself and may do something that you will later regret. At the time you don't realize it and may think that you are capable of making a reasonable decision—your depressed brain is telling you to go ahead with it. His plea was to wait until I was feeling better to make any major life decisions. He was clever, because of course, when you are feeling better, you do not want to give up! So, in this way he got me to keep going and not give up.

Feelings are not fact. Interpretation is not fact. Judgment is not fact. STOP. Look at the facts. Then modify your assessment/interpretation of the situation.

This was a reminder from my therapist when I struggled with believing my distorted thoughts were facts. He reminded me that in depression, negative events are magnified and may dominate your thinking. When you are depressed, you are more likely to believe biased or distorted thoughts are true. Remember: thoughts and feelings are not facts. "Feelings" are created by your thoughts and your interpretations of an event, not by the actual event. Do not confuse feelings and thoughts with facts. Stop and look at the situation in front of you, at the objective facts of the situation. Then make your own assessment based on these facts and not based on any distorted thoughts or feelings. Doing this will bring you to a more realistic view of the situation and cause you less distress.

With depression, feeling "good" is alien and may feel uncomfortable at first. You are not used to it and may feel anxious. The brain sees it as different and "not right," so the tendency is to go back. Don't. You have to push yourself.

Here, a therapist was preparing me for the idea of making progress in therapy. The statement points out that when you are immersed in a mind state like depression for a long time, the brain gets used to it and sees any change from depression as "different." So, when you start to feel good, that new "feel good" state may feel "bad" or uncomfortable to you. You might feel anxious, irritable, and out of sorts. You might feel like retreating back to your old depressed self, which is familiar. Do not allow that to happen. You have to push yourself to get used to the new idea of feeling "good," or at least "better," and eventually you will adjust to it. After all, that is your ultimate goal.

Practice consciously endorsing yourself.

Most people who suffer from depression are very good at negative self-talk. Finding negative, critical things to say about themselves seems to come easily. "I am a loser" and "I am no good" are fairly universal (and inaccurate) beliefs among those who have this illness. But this is not healthy for you. With depression, you have to learn to think about yourself in more positive terms and to give yourself credit for your accomplishments, no matter how small. You have to practice endorsing yourself, on purpose, consciously, and get comfortable having those positive thoughts in your head. Practice saying "I am a good _________" (fill in the blank) several times a day until it feels natural to you. That is what my therapist was trying to say in this statement.

Action precedes motivation.

This is said so often, it has become the mantra of the McLean Hospital Partial Hospital Program. It is meant to address the inertia that comes with depression, the lack of interest in life and in doing things (called anhedonia). What it means is that even when you are depressed and don't feel like doing anything, you should go ahead and do something anyway. Do not wait until you feel like doing it, because in depression, that will not come for a very long time. If you begin to do things, eventually the motivation to do them will follow. It is far easier to stay in bed or on the couch, but that is not in your best interest. Just get going on some small thing and eventually the interest in doing it will follow, and you will become interested in more things. Start with one small thing at a time, and the motivation for doing it will later appear.

Sometimes we experience a combination of physical, emotional, and interpersonal symptoms for such a long time that we don't even recognize them as symptoms. We get used to them and think they are normal.

We discussed this in group therapy years ago, and I just now discovered who wrote it, although it is taken from a book I have not read. I know that it is very true in depression. When symptoms persist for a long time, and your memory gets fuzzy, it is hard to remember what your past self is like. When you get used to the symptoms of longstanding depression, you may think of it as your "normal" self. Remember—that is not true. It is not your normal self. The exercise in chapter 3 is designed to help you define your baseline healthy self and have that as a goal to work toward during your recovery.

Courage doesn't always roar. Sometimes courage is the quiet voice at the end of the day saying "I will try again tomorrow."

This quotation speaks volumes to me. Depression is the kind of illness that requires a lot of courage. Many of us go around with this illness in silence, not mentioning it to any but a few of our closest friends and family, quietly struggling. It takes a lot of effort just to get up each day, to get showered and dressed and try. It takes enormous courage to get up and face another day of depression, of darkness and despair and hopelessness. When you are willing to do that day after day, you have courage unlike any other. You do not have to shout it from the rooftops—you show it quietly by your efforts.

You cannot absorb praise unless you decide to believe and validate what is being said.

A psychiatry resident said this to me one day during one of my major struggles. It is meaningful to those with depression who are overwhelmed with negative self-talk and beliefs that interfere with their ability to receive praise or a compliment. She meant to say that you need to be able to respect and believe what the other person is saying, and validate them, before you can absorb the positive comments they are offering you. That is not easy to do. Once you decide that you can trust and believe the other person, then you can accept their words as accurate and complimentary.

There is Hope because . . . we see you in a different way than you see yourself, and if you were to see yourself as we see you, then you could believe and hope that life could be different.

I was struggling terribly with the idea of having no hope for a life when this wise psychiatrist said this to me. I had to learn and later accept that he saw me in a different way than I saw myself. I was looking through depressed glasses and could not see things as he did, a common problem in depression. And since he saw me differently, he saw a potential for life and hope that I was unable to envision when depressed. I am still learning to see myself through his eyes and the eyes of others who see me this way, to see my potential through their point of view.

That is just the way you have come to regard yourself. It is not necessarily true.

Another physician, who did not know me at all, picked up on the extremely negative view of myself that in depression my brain had come to believe as true. In one brief encounter, she understood that my self-view was an inaccurate distortion. It blew the roof off my long-held premise that the whole world knew me to be as I saw myself when she challenged it. It became a turning point for me, to have someone quickly see through to the "old" me, who was not as my depressed self envisioned. I have to constantly remind myself of her words that this is "not necessarily true."

Helpful Web Sites

National Institute of Mental Health *Information about depression and bipolar disorder, including current research and clinical trials*	www.nimh.nih.gov
American Psychiatric Association *Patient educational information about depression and bipolar disorder*	www.psych.org www.healthyminds.org
American Psychological Association *Patient educational information about depression and bipolar disorder*	www.apa.org
Depression and Bipolar Support Alliance (National Manic Depressive and Depressive Association) *An educational resource for patients with depression, with information on support groups and educational programs*	www.dbsalliance.org
National Alliance for the Mentally Ill *Information about depression and other mental illness*	www.nami.org
PatientsLikeMe *A Web site where you can compare your symptoms and progress in real time with others who share your diagnosis*	www.patientslikeme.com

continued

beyondblue *The Web site of the National Depression Initiative of Australia. Information for patients with depression and bipolar disorder.*	www.beyondblue.org
American Academy of Sleep Medicine *Professional association Web site with some links to patient educational sites*	www.aasmnet.org www.yoursleep.aasmnet.org
National Institutes of Health/NHLBI *Your Guide to Healthy Sleep*	www.nhlbi.nih.gov/health/public/sleep
Centers for Disease Control *Physical Activity Guidelines*	www.cdc.gov/physicalactivity
U.S. Department of Health and Human Services *2008 Physical Activity Guidelines for Americans*	www.health.gov/PAGuidelines
American College of Sports Medicine *Exercise Guidelines*	www.acsm.org
USDA Nutrition and Physical Activity Guidelines *SuperTracker: an online tool to track your daily exercise and calories*	https://www.choosemyplate.gov/SuperTracker/physicalactivitytracker.aspx
U.S. Department of Health and Human Services *Dietary Guidelines for Americans, 2010*	www.health.gov/dietaryguidelines www.choosemyplate.gov
Center for Disease Control *Nutrition*	www.cdc.gov/nutrition

Evaluating Health Information on the Internet

Things to consider	Why is this important?
WHY do I need to evaluate information on the Internet?	You need to be able to find reliable health-related information from trustworthy sources and avoid false or misleading health claims that can be found on the Internet. This means that you must know the sources of the information.
WHO runs the Web site?	You need to know who is responsible for a Web site and its content to be able to evaluate the accuracy and reliability of the information. Look for an "About Us" page and the site's editorial board.
WHO pays for it?	An organization that sponsors, or pays for, a Web site can influence the type and amount of information provided and how it is presented. To evaluate health information, you must first identify any possible *slant or bias* in the material presented. For example, the accuracy of health-related information presented may be influenced by a company's desire to sell a product or service.
What is its ***PURPOSE?***	This is related to who sponsors it. A Web site's goal could be patient education, fundraising, or business. This can present a possible slant or bias. It is important to understand a Web site's purpose when evaluating the information presented.
WHERE does the information come from?	To evaluate the quality and reliability of health information, you need to understand where it comes from. The Web site should identify the following: • The original source of the information—who wrote it. • The source should be a person or organization known to have knowledge and expertise in the area. The site should identify material written by the Web site staff.

continued

Things to consider	Why is this important?
WHERE does the information come from? *(cont'd.)*	• The scientific evidence on which the health information is based, including references for medical facts and statistics (numbers). • Individual opinions as "opinion" and clearly separated from medical information that is based on sound research *(evidence-based)*. • The medical credentials of the author(s) and reviewers to demonstrate that they have expertise in the topic (professional degrees, training, positions).
WHEN was it written?	The information presented should be recent and up-to-date. It should be reviewed regularly to provide you with current information. The most recent *update or review date* should be posted on the Web site.
WHAT different types of health-related material can be found on Web sites?	• *Statements* or facts supported by scientific evidence and research • *Statements* not supported by scientific evidence • *Opinions* by recognized experts on the topic (editorials, comments) • *Opinions* by someone who is not a recognized expert on the topic • *Personal stories* (case reports) • A *combination* of science-based fact and clinical experience by recognized experts in the field
Is the information ***REVIEWED*** by experts?	Health-related Web sites should state whether their information is reviewed before posting, by whom, and ideally how this is done. The process usually involves: • a review of the scientific articles *(evidence)* from respected medical journals • an evaluation of how and why the information is important *(relevance)* • a concise summary of the important points • identification of the authors and their credentials • a review of the material by other medical professionals with expertise in the topic *(peer reviewed)*

Things to consider	Why is this important?
How reliable are the ***LINKS*** to other sites?	Web sites can choose to include links to other Web sites. Their policy could be based on whether other sites meet certain standards or criteria, or they might include only those outside Web sites that pay them money for advertising or to be included.
What about my ***PRIVACY?***	Web sites track what pages in their site you are viewing. They may use this information to improve or modify their site. You may be asked to "register" with the Web site, sometimes for a fee. When you register, you give some *personal information* to the Web site. The site should explain what they do with your personal information. You should understand the Web site's privacy policy. Some sites may sell your information to other companies. Do not register for anything that makes you uncomfortable.
Are users able to ***COMMUNICATE*** with the Web site?	Web sites should offer a way for users (like you) to contact them with questions, problems, and feedback. If there is a chat room or online discussion area, the site should disclose the terms of service, how is it monitored, and by whom.

Source: Adapted in part from U.S. Department of Health and Human Services, "How to Evaluate Health Information on the Internet," www.fda.gov, accessed March 2010, April 2012.

Clues in the Name

Web address ending in:	Type of organization that runs it	Examples
.gov	Federal government-sponsored sites	National Institute of Health
.edu	Schools and other educational institutions	A medical school A university
.org	Noncommercial organizations	American Psychiatric Association A hospital
.com	Commercial organizations (business)	A drug company A bookstore

Books of Interest

Aaron T. Beck, A. John Rush, Brian F. Shaw, and Gary Emery. *Cognitive Therapy of Depression*. Guilford Press, 1979.

David Burns. *Feeling Good: The New Mood Therapy*. Avon Books, 1980.

Mary Ellen Copeland. *Living without Depression and Manic Depression: A Workbook for Maintaining Mood Stability*. New Harbinger Publications, 1994.

Mary Ellen Copeland. *The Depression Workbook: A Guide for Living with Depression and Manic Depression*. New Harbinger Publications, 2001.

Gregg D. Jacobs, Ph.D. *Say Goodnight to Insomnia*. Owl Books, 1998.

Cory F. Newman, Robert L. Leahy, Aaron T. Beck, Noreen A. Reilly-Harrington. *Bipolar Disorder: A Cognitive Therapy Approach*. American Psychological Association, 2002.

Deborah Sichel and Jeanne W. Driscoll. *Women's Moods: What Every Woman Must Know about Hormones, the Brain, and Emotional Health*. Quill, 1999.

Jeffrey E. Young and Janet S. Klosko. *Reinventing Your Life*. Penguin, 1994.

Memoirs

Nell Casey. *Unholy Ghost: Writers on Depression*. William Morrow, 2001.

Kay Redfield Jamison. *Night Falls Fast: Understanding Suicide*. Vintage Books, 2000.

Kay Redfield Jamison. *Touched with Fire: Manic Depressive Illness and the Artistic Temperament*. Free Press, 1993.

Kay Redfield Jamison. *An Unquiet Mind: A Memoir of Mood and Madness*. Vintage Books,1995.

Martha Manning. *Undercurrents: A Life beneath the Surface*. HarperOne, 1995.

William Styron. *Darkness Visible: A Memoir of Madness*. Vintage Books, 1990.

Tracy Thompson. *The Beast: A Journey through Depression*. Plume, 1996.

Meditation

Herbert Benson. *Beyond the Relaxation Response*. Berkeley Books, 1984.

Herbert Benson. *The Relaxation Response*. Harper, 1975, revised 2000.

Jon Kabat-Zinn. *Wherever You Go, There You Are*. Hyperion, 1994.

Communication Skills

Dianna Booher. *Communicate with Confidence: How to Say It Right the First Time*. McGraw-Hill,1994.

Jeff Davidson. *The Complete Idiot's Guide to Assertiveness*. Alpha Books, 1997.

Debra Fine. *The Fine Art of Small Talk*. Small Talk Publishers, 2002.

A. Yeung, G. Feldman, and M. Fava. *Self-Management of Depression: A Manual for Mental Health and Primary Care Professionals*. Cambridge, 2010, app. C.

Conclusion

I have presented a lot of material on managing your mood disorder in the chapters of this book. Starting with the Basics of Mental Health as a foundation for staying healthy and building new skills, I then covered how to identify and monitor your mood disorder and its symptoms. In chapter 3, I described how to identify your baseline healthy self, why it is important, and how it will provide you with a goal for your recovery. Chapter 4 presented you with treatment options and many ways to manage your mood disorder, such as understanding your fluctuations, identifying and monitoring your Warning Signs and Triggers, and maintaining a routine and structure. In chapter 5, I detailed how to respond to your symptoms as they arise by, developing an Action Plan and following Relapse Prevention Strategies.

Chapter 6 described cognitive behavioral therapy, a type of talk therapy particularly useful in depression, with several practical exercises to reinforce the principles of CBT. These CBT exercises help you challenge negative thoughts and avoid negative behaviors, both of which are common in depression. Several strategies were reviewed in chapter 7 to help you get through the difficult times: Coping and Stress, Mindfulness, Distress Tolerance, Communication Skills, Dealing with Family and Friends, Talking with Your Doctor, and Tips for Family and Friends. In chapter 8 I gave you a picture of what life can be like when you follow the recommendations outlined in this book. The last chapter presented additional resources, such as useful books and guidelines for using the Internet to obtain health information.

Do not expect that you will master this material all in one reading. It will take time and practice to learn and incorporate these approaches into your day. Managing your mood disorder means that you learn about the illness and develop strategies to respond to your symptoms. It means that each day you use the methods, strategies, and skills that I have described to deal with the symptoms you have. Managing your illness requires that you monitor your symptoms, challenge negative thoughts, use problem-solving techniques, make adjustments, and avoid negative behaviors. This is a lot to do; in fact, it may feel overwhelming to you right now. With time and practice, however, all steps outlined in this book are possible to accomplish. More important, they will make a difference in how you feel. Work with your treatment providers on this.

Do not be surprised if you need to review sections of the book periodically. Review and practice is how we all learn new skills. This book was designed to introduce the topics relevant to depression one at a time, then to help you reinforce the material by using specific exercises and examples in your life. Last, this book is a reference for reviewing the material later as needed. When you come upon a section that hits home, that is particularly familiar to your situation, sit with it and think about it for a while. Consider how it relates to you. That would be a good example of something for you to discuss with your therapist or physician.

Keep in mind that those patients who participate actively in their care have a better chance of recovery and staying well. So keep working at it. It may take a while for you to notice a change in your mood, and this may understandably affect your motivation to follow the recommendations outlined in the book. Doing so may feel like a struggle. Just remember that action precedes motivation: take that step whether you feel like it today or not.

Good luck!

Glossary

Action Plan for Relapse Prevention • An intervention Action Plan for Relapse Prevention is a written self-care plan to help you deal with a worsening or recurrence of depression. It is a strategy you create with your doctor. You create it in advance and have it ready for the times when your depression symptoms start getting worse. The Action Plan helps you to identify your Symptoms and Warning Signs. It outlines the steps you will take to manage, cope, and distract from the high intensity of a depression or manic episode. The Action Plan also lists the people you will ask to help you during these times: health care providers, family, and friends.

Automatic Negative Thoughts • In depression, the mind quickly jumps to negative thoughts, which usually cause distress. These are the thoughts that are biased in an extreme negative direction, such as "I'm a loser" or "I can't do anything right." This happens because (1) in depression, negative events dominate your thinking, and (2) the depressed mind tends to interpret and distort or twist things negatively, thus creating the negative thoughts. These thoughts happen automatically, not on purpose. Automatic negative thoughts are not an accurate reflection of reality. They are a distortion.

Bipolar Disorder • Bipolar disorder, or manic-depressive disorder, is a relapsing and remitting, treatable mood disorder that has a major effect on daily life. Relapsing and remitting means that the episodes come and go. As with major depression, it is thought to be caused by a dysfunction in the network of neurons (brain cells) in the brain. Bipolar disorder is characterized by periodic episodes of extreme elevated mood or irritability followed by periodic episodes of depression.

Cognitive Behavioral Therapy • Cognitive behavioral therapy (CBT) is a kind of talk therapy (psychotherapy) that addresses the connection between your thoughts, feelings, and actions. In CBT you learn to identify and change thinking patterns that may be distorted, beliefs that are inaccurate, and behaviors that are unhelpful.

Cognitive Distortions • Distortions in your thoughts are errors in thinking that twist your interpretation of an event in different ways. This happens commonly in depression. Cognitive behavioral therapy uses a series of exercises to challenge and replace the negative and distorted thoughts that accompany depression.

Coping • Coping strategies are the steps you can actively take to lessen the effects of stress and decrease your vulnerability to stressors. Coping includes problem solving, self-soothing, relaxation, distraction, humor, Mindfulness meditation, and other techniques.

Depression • Depression is a relapsing and remitting but treatable illness. Relapsing and remitting means that the episodes come and go. It affects your thoughts, feelings, behaviors, relationships, activities, interests, and many other aspects of life. Depression is thought to involve a dysfunction in the network of neurons (brain cells) in the brain. This may happen when certain life experiences occur in a susceptible person.

Distorted Thinking • Distortions in your thoughts are errors in thinking that twist your interpretation of an event in different ways. Cognitive behavioral therapy uses a series of exercises to challenge and replace the negative and distorted thoughts that accompany depression.

Distress Tolerance • Distress Tolerance is the ability to tolerate extreme distress for a short period, until the crisis of the moment passes. It is a strategy to get through a brief difficult time when you cannot change the situation. Distress Tolerance strategies include using skills to distract yourself, soothe yourself, provide solace, and improve the difficult moment.

Mood Disorders • Mood disorders is a term that includes major depression and bipolar disorder, conditions of the brain that involve a disturbance in your mood or state of mind.

Psychomotor Agitation • Psychomotor agitation is a symptom best described as a combination of excessive physical and mental (or cognitive) activity occurring at the same time. It is usually without purpose and is nonproductive. This agitation can be a symptom of some mental health conditions, such as in the mania or hypomania of bipolar disorder.

Relapse Prevention • Relapse Prevention is an effective daily approach to help you minimize the chance of a relapse, or return of symptoms, occurring and to help you stay well. Relapse Prevention means that you identify and respond promptly to changes in your Warning Signs, Triggers, or Symptoms. This helps you to intervene when an important change in your emotional health may be happening. Early identification and intervention can prevent your episode from worsening.

Sleep Hygiene • Sleep Hygiene refers to the personal habits, behaviors, and environmental (home) conditions that can help you get the sleep you need. Attending to these habits can help improve the quality and the quantity of your sleep. It is important to pay attention to Sleep Hygiene principles during episodes of depression, when your sleep patterns are likely to be disrupted.

Triggers • Triggers are events or circumstances that may cause you distress and lead to an increase in your symptoms of depression.

Warning Signs • Warning Signs are distinct changes from your baseline that precede an episode of depression or mania.

References

Introduction

T. Bodenheimer, K. Lorig, H. Holman, et al. Patient self-management of chronic disease in primary care. JAMA 2002;288(19):2469–75.

E. Ludman, W. Katon, T. Bush, et al. Behavioral factors associated with symptom outcomes in a primary care-based depression prevention intervention trial. Psychol Med 2003;33:1061–70.

William Styron. *Darkness Visible: A Memoir of Madness*. Vintage Books, 1990.

A. Yeung, G. Feldman, and M. Fava. *Self-Management of Depression: A Manual for Mental Health and Primary Care Professionals*. Cambridge, 2010.

Chapter 1. Mental Health Basics

Sleep

American Academy of Sleep Medicine. *Sleep Hygiene*. www.yoursleep.aasmnet.org, accessed April 2012.

F. K. Goodwin and K. R. Jamison. *Manic-Depressive Illness*. 2nd ed. Oxford, 2007.

National Institutes of Health, National Heart, Lung, and Blood Institute. *Your Guide to Healthy Sleep*. 2005, revised 2011. www.nhlbi.nih.gov/health/public/sleep, accessed April 2012.

Sleep Diary. Adapted from NIH/NHLBI, *Your Guide to Healthy Sleep*. 2005, revised 2011. www.nhlbi.nih.gov/health/public/sleep, accessed April 2012.

N. Tsuno, S. Besset, and K. Ritchie. Sleep and depression. J Clin Psychiatry 2005;66(10):1254–69.

J. W. Winkelman and D. T. Plante, ed. *Foundations of Psychiatric Sleep Medicine*. Cambridge, 2011.

Nutrition

L. M. Bodnar and K. L. Wisner. Nutrition and depression: Implications for improving mental health among childbearing-aged women. Biol Psych. 2005;58(9):679–85.

M. Fava. Weight gain and antidepressants. J Clin Psychiatry 2000;61 (suppl 11):37–41.

R.M.A. Hirschfeld. Long-term side effects of SSRI's: Sexual dysfunction and weight gain. J Clin Psychiatry 2003;64(suppl 18):20–24.

F. N. Jacka, J. A. Pasco, A. Mykletun, et al. Association of western and traditional diets with depression and anxiety in women. Am J Psychiatry 2010;167(3):305–11.

S. J. Nielsen and B. M. Popkin. Patterns and trends in food portion sizes, 1977–1998. JAMA. 2003;289(4):450–53.

G. I. Papakostas. Limitations of contemporary antidepressants: Tolerability. J Clin Psychiatry 2007;68(suppl 10):11–17.

National Institutes of Health, National Heart, Lung, and Blood Institute. Food Portion sizes: Serving Size Card. http://hp2010.nhlbihin.net/portion/servingcard7.pdf, accessed April 2012.

U.S. Department of Agriculture. ChooseMyPlate.gov. www.choosemyplate.gov, accessed April 2012.

U.S. Department of Agriculture and U.S. Department of Health and Human Services. *Dietary Guidelines for Americans, 2010*. 7th edition. Washington, DC: U.S. Government Printing Office, December 2010. www.health.gov/DietaryGuidelines/, accessed April 2012.

Exercise

M. Babyak, J. A. Blumenthal, S. Herman, et al. Exercise treatment for major depression: Maintenance of therapeutic benefit at 10 months. Psychosomatic Medicine 2000;62:633–38.

Centers for Disease Control and Prevention. Physical Activity. www.cdc.gov/physicalactivity, accessed April 2012.

C. W. Cotman, N. C. Berchtold, and L. A. Christie. Exercise builds brain health: Key roles of growth factor cascades and inflammation. Trends in Neurosciences 2007;30(9):464–72.

A. L. Dunn, M. H. Trivedi, J. B. Kampert, et al. Exercise treatment for depression: Efficacy and dose response. Am J Prev Med 2005;28(1):1–8.

C. E. Garber, B. Blissmer, M. R. Deschenes, et al. Position Stand: Quantity and quality of exercise for developing and maintaining cardiorespiratory, musculoskeletal, and neuromotor fitness in apparently healthy adults: Guidelines for prescribing exercise. Medicine and Science in Sports and Exercise 2011;43(7)1334–59.

G. E. Mead, W Morley, P Campbell, et al. Exercise for depression. Cochrane Database of Sytematic Reviews (3):CD004366, 2009.

M. H. Trivedi, T. L. Greer, T. S. Church, et al. Exercise as an Augmentation treatment for nonremitted major depressive disorder: A randomized, parallel dose comparison. J Clin Psychiatry 2011;72(5):677–84.

U.S. Department of Health and Human Services. Physical Activity Guidelines for Americans. 2008. www.health.gov/paguidelines, accessed April 2012.

A. Yeung, G. Feldman, and M. Fava. *Self-Management of Depression: A Manual for Mental Health and Primary Care Professionals*. Cambridge, 2010, chap. 5.

Routine and Structure

E. Frank. Interpersonal and social rhythm therapy: A means of improving depression and preventing relapse in bipolar disorder. J Clin Psychology: In Session 2007;63(5):463–73.

E. Frank, S. Hlastala, A. Ritenour, et al. Inducing lifestyle regularity in recovering bipolar disorder patients: Results from the maintenance therapies in bipolar disorder protocol. Biol Psychiatry 1997;41:1165–73.

Isolation

K. S. Kendler, J. Myers, and C. A. Prescott. Sex differences in the relationship between social support and risk for major depression: A longitudinal study of opposite-sex twin pairs. Am J Psychiatry 2005;162(2):250–56.

Chapter 2. Mood Disorders

American Psychiatric Association. *Diagnostic and Statistical Manual of Mental Disorders*. 4th ed., text revision. American Psychiatric Association, 2000.

A. T. Beck and B. A. Alford. *Depression: Causes and Treatment*. University of Pennsylvania Press, 2009.

M. Fava, J. E. Alpert, C. N. Carmin, et al. Clinical correlates and symptom patterns of anxious depression among patients with major depressive disorder in STAR*D. Psychol Med 2004;34:1299–1308.

F. K. Goodwin and K. R. Jamison. *Manic-Depressive Illness*. 2nd ed. Oxford, 2007.

D. Sichel and J. W. Driscoll. *Women's Mood's: What Every Woman Must Know about Hormones, the Brain, and Emotional Health*. Quill, 1999.

Fatigue and Depression

L. M. Arnold. Understanding fatigue in major depressive disorder and other medical disorders. Psychosomatics 2008;49(3):185–90.

D. S. Baldwin and G. I. Papakostas. Symptoms of fatigue and sleepiness in major depressive disorder. J Clin Psych 2006;67(suppl 6):9–15.

A. A. Nierenberg, B. R. Keefe, V. C. Leslie, et al. Residual symptoms in depressed patients who respond acutely to fluoxetine. J Clin Psych 1999;60(4):221–25.

A. A. Nierenberg, M. M. Husain, M. H. Trivedi, et al. Residual symptoms after remission of major depressive disorder with citalopram and risk of relapse: A STAR*D report. Psychol Med 2010;40:41–50.

A. Tylee, M. Gastpar, J-P. Lepine, et al., on behalf of the DEPRES Steering Committee. DEPRES II (Depression Research in European Society II): A patient survey of the symptoms, disability and current management of depression in the community. Int Clin Psychopharm 1999;14(3):139–51.

Chapter 4. Managing Your Mood Disorder

A. T. Beck and B. A. Alford. *Depression: Causes and Treatment*. University of Pennsylvania Press, 2009.

G. A. Fava, C. Rafanelli, S. Grandi, et al. Prevention of recurrent depression with cognitive behavioral therapy. Arch Gen Psych 1998;55:816–20.

F. K. Goodwin and K. R. Jamison. *Manic-Depressive Illness*. 2nd ed. Oxford, 2007.

R. Harley, S. Sprich, Jacobo M. Safran, and M. Fava. Adaptation of dialectical behavioral therapy skills training group for treatment-resistant depression. J Nerv Mental Dis 2008;196(2):136–43.

E.H.B. Lin, M. Von Korff, E. J. Ludman, et al. Enhancing adherence to prevent depression relapse in primary care. Gen Hosp Psychiatry 2003;25(3):303–10.

M. M. Linehan. *Cognitive-Behavioral Treatment of Borderline Personality Disorder*. Guilford Press, 1993.

E. Ludman, W. Katon, T. Bush, et al. Behavioral factors associated with symptom outcomes in a primary care-based depression prevention intervention trial. Psychol Med 2003;33:1061–70.

A. A. Nierenberg, T. J. Petersen, and J. A. Alpert. Prevention of relapse and recurrence in depression: The role of long-term pharmacotherapy and psychotherapy. J Clin Psychiatry 2003;64(suppl 15):13–17.

E. S. Paykel, J. Scott, J. D. Teasdale, et al. Prevention of relapse in residual depression by cognitive therapy. Arch Gen Psych 1999;56:829–35.

T. J. Petersen. Enhancing the efficacy of antidepressants with psychotherapy. Journ Psychopharmacology 2006;20(3):19–28.

C. S. Richards and M. G. Perri, ed. *Relapse Prevention for Depression*. American Psychological Association, 2010.

G. E. Simon, E.H.B. Lin, W. Katon, et al. Outcomes of "inadequate" antidepressant treatment. J Gen Int Med 1995;10(12):663–70.

J. D. Teasdale, Z. V. Segal, J.M.G. Williams, et al. Prevention of relapse/recurrence in major depression by mindfulness-based cognitive therapy. J Consulting Clin Psych 2000;8(4):615–23.

M. H. Trivedi, E.H.B. Lin, and W. J. Katon. Consensus recommendations for improving adherence, self-management, and outcomes in patients with depression. CNS Spectrums 2007;12:8(Suppl 13):1–27.

A. Yeung, G. Feldman, and M. Fava. *Self-Management of Depression: A Manual for Mental Health and Primary Care Professionals*. Cambridge, 2010.

Chapter 5. Relapse Prevention

American Psychiatric Association. *Diagnostic and Statistical Manual of Mental Disorders*. 4th ed., text revision. American Psychiatric Association, 2000.

A. T. Beck and B. A. Alford. *Depression: Causes and Treatment*. University of Pennsylvania Press, 2009.

G. A. Fava, C. Rafanelli, S. Grandi, et al. Prevention of recurrent depression with cognitive behavioral therapy. Arch Gen Psych 1998;55:816–20.

E. Frank. Interpersonal and social rhythm therapy: A means of improving

depression and preventing relapse in bipolar disorder. J Clin Psychology: In Session 2007;63(5):463–73.
E. Frank, S. Hlastala, A. Ritenour, et al. Inducing lifestyle regularity in recovering bipolar disorder patients: Results from the maintenance therapies in bipolar disorder protocol. Biol Psychiatry 1997;41:1165–73.
E. Ludman, W. Katon, T. Bush, et al. Behavioral factors associated with symptom outcomes in a primary care-based depression prevention intervention trial. Psychol Med 2003;33:1061–70.
E. S. Paykel, J. Scott, J. D. Teasdale, et al. Prevention of relapse in residual depression by cognitive therapy. Arch Gen Psych 1999;56:829–35.
T. J. Petersen. Enhancing the efficacy of antidepressants with psychotherapy. Journ Psychopharmacology 2006;20(3):19–28.
C. S. Richards and M. G. Perri, ed. *Relapse Prevention for Depression*. American Psychological Association, 2010.
J. D. Teasdale, Z. V. Segal, J.M.G. Williams, et al. Prevention of relapse/recurrence in major depression by mindfulness-based cognitive therapy. J Consulting Clin Psych 2000;8(4):615–23.

Chapter 6. Cognitive Behavioral Therapy

A. T. Beck, A. J. Rush, B. F. Shaw, and G. Emery. *Cognitive Therapy of Depression*. Guilford Press, 1979.
A. T. Beck and B. A. Alford. *Depression: Causes and Treatment*. University of Pennsylvania Press, 2009.
David Burns. *Feeling Good: The New Mood Therapy*. Avon Books, 1980.
F. K. Goodwin and K. R. Jamison. *Manic-Depressive Illness*. 2nd ed. Oxford, 2007.
D. M. Sudak. Cognitive behavioral therapy for depression. Psychiatric Clin N Am 2012;35:99–110.

Chapter 7. Strategies to Get You Through the Tough Times

Herbert Benson. *The Relaxation Response*. Harper, 1975, revised 2000.
William Styron. *Darkness Visible: A Memoir of Madness*. Vintage Books, 1990.

Mindfulness

Jon Kabat-Zinn. *Wherever You Go, There You Are*. Hyperion, 1994.

M. M. Linehan. *Skills Training Manual for Treating Borderline Personality Disorder*. Guilford Press, 1993.

Z. V. Segal, J.M.G. Williams, and J. D. Teasdale. *Mindfulness-Based Cognitive Therapy for Depression*. Guilford Press, 2002.

Distress Tolerance

M. M. Linehan. *Cognitive-Behavioral Treatment of Borderline Personality Disorder*. Guilford Press, 1993.

M. M. Linehan. *Skills Training Manual for Treating Borderline Personality Disorder*. Guilford Press, 1993.

Communication Skills

Dianna Booher. *Communicate with Confidence: How to Say It Right the First Time*. McGraw-Hill, 1994.

Jeff Davidson. *The Complete Idiot's Guide to Assertiveness*. Alpha Books, 1997.

Debra Fine. *The Fine Art of Small Talk*. Small Talk Publishers, 2002.

A. Yeung, G. Feldman, and M. Fava. *Self-Management of Depression: A Manual for Mental Health and Primary Care Professionals*. Cambridge, 2010, app. C.

Index